Advance Praise for Madison & Vine

"A superb analysis of the intersection of Madison and Vine. Donaton thoroughly explores it in a concise, well-documented style. This convergence is the future financial model of the entertainment and advertising industries."

—*Mark Burnett, Creator/Executive Producer of "The Apprentice" and "Survivor"*

"Scott Donaton does more than lay out a road map of the future. He makes you smell the sweat on the upper lip of every advertising executive trying to save his bacon in the scary, dangerous intersection of our greatest cultural forces—advertising and the entertainment media that helps this nation sell itself to itself. This book explicates the inexplicable, sure, but it also fills your imagination with the metallic taste of fear that grips the buyer, the agent, the programming executive whose next car could be a used Kia if they don't figure out what the hell is going on. A word to those who want some action in this crazily converging techno-centric world: read this book or be left behind."

—*Stanley Bing, bestselling author of* What Would Machiavelli Do? *and* FORTUNE *magazine columnist*

"Scott Donaton was one of the first to call attention to this space and now he's written the definitive book about the mutual benefit that happens when filmmakers and marketers collaborate."

—*Harvey Weinstein, President, Miramax Film Corp.*

"Unique and insightful, Scott provides an insider's look into the evolving business models of entertainment and advertising. *Madison & Vine* has forced execs to reconsider the power of branded entertainment and serves as a guide for all involved to wake up and create strategically streamlined marketing programs that make sure dollars deliver on ROl. That, or be left behind."

—*Donny Deutsch, Chairman and CEO, Deutsch Inc.*

"Scott Donaton knows the most important thing there is to know about the media business and that's what's happening to the advertising business. The traditional advertising model, which has for so long ruled the media, is deconstructing—in fact it's blowing up in our faces. This is such a frightening development that almost nobody has been willing to think about it— except Scott Donaton. In this sharp, witting, and prescient book, he imagines the future of our business. It's a new game."

—*Michael Wolff, author,* Autumn of the Moguls, *and* Vanity Fair *columnist*

"If you don't work in the so-called media businesses, this book is a sharp, lucid, knowledgeable and entertaining primer on one large swath of the near future— that is, why and how entertainment and advertising are being transformed (and in some cases rendered obsolete) by new technologies and new sensibilities. And if you do work in the media businesses, this book might help you figure out what you ought to do with the rest of your life before it's too late."

—*Kurt Andersen, bestselling author, editor, and host of NPR's* Studio 360

Madison & Vine

Why the Entertainment and Advertising Industries Must Converge to Survive

Scott Donaton

McGraw-Hill

New York Chicago San Francisco Lisbon London
Madrid Mexico City Milan New Delhi San Juan
Seoul Singapore Sydney Toronto

1 2 3 4 5 6 7 8 9 0   DOC/DOC   0 9 8 7 6 5 (PBK)
3 4 5 6 7 8 9 0   DOC/DOC   0 9 8 7 6 5 4 (HC)

ISBN 0-07-146216-3(PBK)
ISBN 0-07-143684-7(HC)

First McGraw-Hill paperback edition published in 2005.

McGraw-Hill books are available at special quantity discounts to use as premiums and sales promotions, or for use in corporate training programs. For more information, please write to the Director of Special Sales, McGraw-Hill Professional, Two Penn Plaza, New York, NY 10121-2298. Or contact your local bookstore.

This book is printed on recycled, acid-free paper containing a minimum of 50% recycled, de-inked fiber.

For Molly, Jack and Liam

Contents

Preface

My earliest words on the convergence of entertainment and advertising were harsh ones. It was a topic I had brushed against a couple of times in my column, but never as directly as in April 2002, when I wrote a piece in Advertising Age that carried the headline, "When Advertising Mixes with Hollywood, Cheap Alloy Results."

"Marketers are hot on the idea of product placement," I wrote. "They've convinced themselves that giving it a new name (product integration) qualifies it as a creative concept rather than a recycled device from TV's earliest days. In assuming control over storylines and media content, their motivation is not to have a more engaging dialogue with consumers; it is the fear that personal-video recorders will make 30-second ads obsolete. How do you connect to consumers who give you a brusque technological brush-off?"

"Something is missing from the equation in the new marketing math: the consumer," I also noted.

The intention of this viewpoint piece was not to devalue the concept of alliances between the advertising industry and entertainment companies. Rather, the piece was intended as a warning to those who were headed into the space—to alert them that they couldn't afford to lose sight of the audience's needs in trying to satisfy their own. The media revolution that was underway was all about the empowerment of consumers. Already savvy and able to quickly detect blatant attempts at manipulation, they now also had the power to banish such fare, to easily reject any ads, movies, TV shows, or music offerings that seemed designed more to sell product than to entertain or inform.

The column was also a challenge to the entertainment and advertising industries to be more creative in their responses to the immense changes that were ripping through their business models. Many early attempts at "product integration" were not organic in any way; they were uninspired, sore-thumb product placements that spoiled the TV shows and films in which they appeared. The advertising business was facing incredible change, and its initial response didn't seem worthy of the challenge.

To my surprise, some readers interpreted the column not as a caution but as a blatant rejection of the intersection of advertising and entertainment. In retrospect, that turned out to be a good thing, since several of those people, particularly from the Hollywood side, made it their personal mission to win me over to their optimistic view of the marriage, or at least to better articulate their positions. Those discussions and debates, in conference rooms and over breakfasts, lunches, and dinners with entertainment types from Los Angeles, ad executives from New York, and marketers from around the country, helped to shape my views on what was happening and why it was important. There were true believers on all sides who saw opportunities to enhance both consumer brands and the entertainment experience by combining the best of both. Their long-standing distrust and resistance to deepening their relationship had been broken down by the common fear that digital technologies, among other factors, posed a significant threat to their traditional business models.

Something real and often exciting is happening at this intersection of advertising and entertainment, although even believers are advised to maintain a healthy skepticism. There have been missteps already, and there will be many more along the way—some of them no doubt troubling enough to threaten the credibility of the entire concept. These are also the earliest days, and the space is only now being defined. It will look very different a few years from now, and the key for those whose futures may depend on it will be to remain flexible, willing to change and evolve.

The nature of such change can be difficult to predict. In the fall of 1993, *Ad Age* introduced a weekly section that we called Interactive Media & Marketing. (I became the section's editor early the following year.) The name was broad enough to cover various new communications forms and flexible enough to evolve with the technologies. At first, its focus was on interactive, or two-way, TV, an expensive, before-its-time concept that promised to let viewers interact with the programs they watched, ordering the sweater worn by a character in a sitcom or altering plot lines at the touch of a button on their remotes. Next came dial-up online services such as Prodigy, CompuServe, and America Online, each of which then had fewer than 1 million subscribers (today, AOL has more than 25 million, although that number has been declining as more people switch to broadband high-speed Internet connections through their telephone or cable service). Other forms of "emerging media" included interactive kiosks, which spit out recipes and coupons to grocery store shoppers, and multimedia magazines distributed on CD-ROMs that featured text, videos, and music. More than a year after the section was launched, it began to cover the Internet and the commercial marketplace known as the World Wide Web. A year later, pretty much everything except the Web had fallen away, and the Web had emerged as a revolutionary force in media and marketing (if a severely overhyped one).

By the year 2000, the interactive space bore little resemblance to the interactive space in the year 1993. In 2004, it looks nothing like it did in 2000. The key was to follow the story, to change when it did.

The Madison & Vine space at its infancy looks quite similar to the interactive space a decade earlier. Once again, there is hype that threatens to undermine a real underlying base. Once again, there are more questions than answers. Once again, there is a new community being formed, made up in many cases of people who had never before done business with one another but who now find their fates entwined. This set of circumstances seems ideal for journalism, for a platform through which to introduce members of the community to one another, to define the issues and answer the questions, to differentiate hype from reality.

In the summer of 2002—just a few months after the "cheap alloy" column—*Advertising Age* introduced a weekly email newsletter called *Madison & Vine* (named for the avenues in New York City and Hollywood that are often used as casual shorthand for the advertising and entertainment industries, respectively). There was also regular coverage of the topic in the pages of *Ad Age*—many of those stories, and several of my columns, were relied on to write this book—and in early 2003, we successfully hosted our first Madison & Vine conference.

This book seemed the next logical step. In its pages, I've tried to tell the story of this phenomenon and to outline the revolutionary changes that are sweeping the advertising industry and various segments of the entertainment industry—primarily film, TV, and music. The traditional models of these businesses are under pressure, and one of the most significant ways in which the businesses are coping with change is through alliances that benefit all sides. I've spent a lot of time talking to people representing different parts of this world, leaders in this space from various industries. Their views and stories are represented in these pages, and hopefully the larger story makes itself evident through their individual tales.

It's not clear what Madison & Vine alliances might look like a decade from now, but they will be around—a viable solution to the emerging business challenges. Digital technologies that empower individuals will permanently transform communications in all its forms. Figuring out how won't be easy, but it should be an incredible adventure.

—*Scott Donaton*
January 2004

Acknowledgments

When people ask me why I wanted to write this book, I have two answers: first, it's a topic I'm passionate about; and, second, I wanted to see, well, if I could write a book. It appears that I could, but of course such things are never accomplished without considerable help. So I'd like to thank all those who helped me, especially those I've invariably forgotten to mention below.

First, Rance Crain, owner and president of Crain Communications and editor in chief of Advertising Age, which was founded by his father, G.D. Crain, Jr., in 1930. Rance, along with Gloria Scoby, David Klein and Jill Manee, supported my Madison & Vine proposal from the start. The brand, and this book, wouldn't exist without their decision to invest in my idea. All are also partners from whom I've learned much during my career.

My agent, Cynthia Manson, bought into the book concept before I had even figured out how to sell it, and was tireless in getting the deal done and staying with me through every step along the way. My editor at McGraw-Hill, Mary Glenn, and her team, provided both the structure and creative freedom needed to get this story told.

Hank Kim, the editor of the Madison & Vine newsletter, was a great sounding board, and the newsletter a terrific resource. My assistant, Brooke Capps, helped me in a thousand ways big and small, most valuably as a researcher. Elicia Greenberg spent considerable time and energy figuring out how to make a success out of the Madison & Vine brand in all its iterations. Jonah Bloom, Judann Pollack and Ann Marie Kerwin are great friends and editors. They keep Ad Age running on time and in the right direction, giving me the ability and confidence to stretch.

There were any number of friends and colleagues who provided advice, support and encouragement along the way, professionally and personally. They include Bob Garfield and Randall Rothenberg, journalists and authors whose work I greatly admire. Randy was one of the first to recognize the impact digital technologies would have on the marketing and media businesses. Mitch Kanner made me a believer in branded entertainment, and was always there when I needed help getting a story straight or finding the right person to interview.

Laura Petrecca was my first reader (and, therefore, first editor), one of the first to preorder the book online and an awesome friend. She believed in my ability to get the book done before I did.

Finally, I want to thank my family, especially my amazing children, Molly, Jack and Liam, my mother, Ann Goffredo, and sister, Lee Ann Pesta. With their support, I know anything is possible.

Chapter 1

Out of Order

*"[It's] a magnitude and urgency of change
that isn't evolutionary—it's
transformational. . . . If a new model isn't
developed, the old one will simply collapse."*

STEVEN J. HEYER, PRESIDENT-COO, COCA-COLA CO.
KEYNOTE ADDRESS, *AD AGE* MADISON & VINE CONFERENCE
FEB. 5, 2003

With those words, the revolution was officially underway.

People knew it was coming and wanted to believe it was real, this new-old alliance of the entertainment and advertising industries that promised to repair, or at least bandage, their wounded business models. It's why hundreds of industry leaders were packed tight, standing room only, in the ballroom of the fabled, and still glamorous, Beverly Hills Hotel on a sun-drenched February morning.

The room buzzed with the chatter of a broad cross section of players from all areas of the entertainment and advertising industries. Big-brand advertising executives mingled with studio marketing wizards; heads of music labels chatted up attorneys; talent agents swapped business cards with TV network honchos; West Coast consultants elbowed through the crowd to get face time with East Coast ad agency bosses. In an unintentional symbolic underscoring of the day's theme, roughly half the crowd had traveled to the hotel by car from their homes by the Pacific Ocean or in the valley; the other half had arrived on airplanes, mostly from New York.

Madison, meet Vine.

These East Coast and West Coast influentials, having happily carved up the country for their respective industries decades ago (and having mostly stayed put on their own turf since then), suddenly found themselves at the same intersection, fierce competitors who were being forced to collaborate. Underlying it all was fear. These were all industries whose business models had cracked and in some cases were completely broken. Talent agents. Music executives. Ad agents. Marketers. Filmmakers. Network chieftains. Their bottom lines all threatened by consumer-empowering technologies.

This is the reason that Turner Broadcasting's then-CEO Jamie Kellner half-jokingly labeled an executive from TiVo—a maker of devices that allow viewers to bypass commercials easily—the "Antichrist" and warned that TV networks could be forced to switch from an ad model to a subscription model, getting consumers to cough up the money that advertisers won't spend when their spots are being zapped into oblivion.

The most interesting battle was between talent agencies and ad agencies. Talent agencies traditionally had negotiated deals for actors, directors, writers, and musicians, but were now trying to position themselves as corporate America's gateway to the entertainment community. Ad agencies, the makers of commercials and buyers of media time for advertisers, tended to bristle at any threat to their strategic role with clients and groused that talent agents aren't accountable (they get paid a fixed fee when an actor lands a film role, and so their compensation has no relation to the ultimate success or failure of the film) and have no understanding of consumer brands. Yet marketers were demanding collaboration without excuses, and the resulting tension was palpable.

The name Madison & Vine is a colorful description of the intersection of content (TV shows, films, music CDs, video games, and so on) and commerce (represented by advertising), but this is not merely about product placements or a fearful response to the perils facing the 30-second spot. It is nothing short of a reinvention of the business of marketing communications, a fundamental transformation from an intrusion-based marketing economy to an invitation-based model.

This power shift will force changes in how marketing communications are defined, created, distributed, and consumed. It will make brands, and it will destroy brands. Innovators who respect the transfer of control and invite consumers to interact with brands on their own terms will survive. Resisters will be trampled. As the CEO of one ad agency told me, "Nobody wants to live through that period of disruption."

From my vantage point, nobody has a choice.

The several hundred attendees of the Beverly Hills conference were there, in part, to convince one another that this was real, and also to begin to define the boundaries of this new community, to seek out a common language and a common currency system. Some sensed the opportunity to get rich; others merely wanted to avoid obsolescence.

In advertising and entertainment, it's a truism that money talks. So when Steven J. Heyer took the stage, everyone was eager to listen. It was one thing for a talent agent, a consultant, or some other intermediary, or even a journalist, to say that this movement, this convergence, was real. It was quite another for Steve Heyer to say it. Because Steve Heyer was one of them, a man who had sat on all sides of the industry table, at times a buyer, at times a seller. A former president of the ad agency giant Young & Rubicam, a former president of cable TV power Turner Broadcasting, which at that time was Ted Turner's arm of the Time Warner empire, Heyer was now the president and chief operating officer of Coca-Cola Company and a potential heir to the CEO's throne, charged with oversight of one of the world's most valuable brands.

And he had a budget. Coca-Cola spends more than half a billion dollars a year just on advertising in the United States, making it one of the top 60 advertisers in the nation, and it spends at least as much again to market its flavored sugar-waters in other countries around the world. And those figures represent just what it spends to advertise on TV, in magazines, on billboards, and for other forms of so-called measured media expenditures, meaning that its total global marketing outlay—which also includes spending on such things as public relations and direct marketing—is significantly higher. So when Heyer said that this was real—no ifs, ands, or buts—and backed his words with the enormous clout of his marketing budget, that was all the external validation that was needed. It was indisputably real. The revolution had begun.

This is a story about the future and the past. Mostly, though, it's an urgent tale about the present; about glamorous, high-profile industries coming together to ensure their mutual survival.

It's about consumers who have been empowered by the Internet and devices such as TiVo recorders and iPod music players, digital storage systems that turn what had been passive consumers into their own network TV programmers, their own radio disc jockeys.

It's about the dismantling and reinvention of business models and the resulting alliances and rivalries—often between the same sets of companies. These are boldface industries—the glamorous businesses of making movies, TV shows, music, and advertising—that are facing change and that need to confront the dangers of clinging to and defending entrenched practices that have outlived their usefulness.

The business models of the advertising and entertainment industries have been badly damaged (in some cases destroyed) and need to be overhauled to ensure the industries' future. As these business models collapse, there is a scramble to create a new model, one in which advertisers and the entertainment industries prop themselves against each other so that neither falls down (even if neither is fully upright or able to stand independently). To get to this point, to ensure their mutual survival, these industries have to overcome distrust, often-divergent agendas, and creative conflicts and collaborate by forming alliances that benefit both.

The outcome will affect big business and popular culture, and it will be determined as much by the couch potato as by the corporate CEO.

On the most basic level, this is a story about the disruptive, transformational powers of new technologies. But it's not a technology tale. Most of the principal players are anything but geeks. Some of them barely know how to turn on their computers, relying on personal assistants to print out copies of their emails, which they read in the backs of their Town Cars as they are chauffeured home from work each day, scribbling their replies in the margins for someone else to type in and send out the following morning.

But while they're not all computer-savvy, they are (for the most part) smart. All the players in these worlds have a clear and discomfiting understanding that new technologies—the Internet, digital music devices, personal digital assistants, and digital video recorders—represent threats to their familiar ways of life and are changing their businesses forever. It's their responses that vary.

There are those whose battle cry is, "Not on my watch!" They know that change is inevitable, but they want to do their best to delay it, at least until after their own retirement, when it will become someone else's problem. "It won't happen in my lifetime" is an oft-repeated mantra. These people are motivated by a desire to protect their own jobs. Not surprisingly, there are a lot of them. They search eagerly for, and latch onto, any signs that the new technologies are a passing fancy that will never gain mainstream consumer acceptance. They cheer any stumble by the companies that threaten them. They turn to the courts and threaten to bring in dreaded government regulators in attempts to trip up their rivals. Their tactics rarely succeed in anything more than the slightest of delays—speed bumps rather than potholes or roadblocks. (Lawsuits filed against Replay, a competitor to TiVo didn't stop personal video recorders; lawsuits against Napster shut down that service but didn't stop the illegal downloading of music.) For executives nearing retirement, a slight delay is sometimes enough.

But the business world is populated by forward thinkers as well, those who want to get ahead of change and play a role in defining and creating the new world order. To some degree, the gap is generational, but that's probably not a fair generalization. There are young executives who are as much in denial about the collapse of the world they know as their counterparts who are less than a year from the gold watch. And there are CEOs whose seventieth birthdays are right around the corner who record TV shows on digital storage devices, cram their iPod music players with thousands of tunes to motivate them while they jog in Central Park, and turn their considerable experience and wisdom to the task of figuring out the future.

The key change is a transfer of power from those who make and distribute entertainment products to those who consume them. In other words, power is moving from the film studios, TV networks, music labels, and ad agencies to the guy on the couch with a remote control in his hand, the woman buying movie tickets at the local theater, and the teen downloading music from the Internet. The consumer has been empowered and liberated. To put it in the simplest terms, that changes everything. "Like most revolutions—including the one that involved taxation without representation, the Boston Tea Party and the Continental Congress—this one is about control," *Advertising Age* columnist Randall Rothenberg, an early convert to the cult of TiVo, wrote in 2000.

To understand what a radical overturning of the traditional model this shift in control represents, it's important to understand the traditional model. Entertainment and advertising have historically been based on an invasive model. For more than 50 years, TV was a passive medium—viewers sat in front of the TV while programming and advertising messages were pushed at them. The networks, local stations, and advertisers scheduled what consumers were going to see and when—decided, effectively, how viewers would consume their messages.

This model is dependent on consumers' being willing to cede control to others, to sit back and accept what comes their way. For a long time, they had no choice.

But this is the age of the empowered consumer, and that means that entertainment providers and advertisers have to move from a model based on intrusion to one that is dependent on invitation. The consumer is now in control of how and when messages reach him or her, and if the consumer doesn't want your message, it's gone. The push model is dead. Consumers now "pull" media toward them and have the ability to screen out those things that they don't want, whether by using digital technology to zap a commercial or simply by choosing a different channel from a menu of hundreds of programming options.

In the not-so-distant past, if you wanted to watch the network evening news, it meant one thing: You had to be at home in front of the television set at the exact time the network was showing the evening news, typically around 6:30 p.m., the mythical post-dinner period of the now-mythical traditional American family. The news was scheduled mostly around Dad, who by that time presumably would be ready to settle in front of the set with his pipe and slippers, newspaper in his lap, loyal dog curled at his feet. Mom, presumably, was washing the dishes while the kids finished up their homework or changed into their pajamas.

The reality, of course, looks nothing like that. In many American families, Mom and Dad both work outside the home, and there's a good chance that one or both of them will arrive later than 6:30. Homes have multiple TV sets, each able to receive hundreds of channels. The kids are in their rooms eating takeout and watching cable channels dedicated to cartoons or cute animals while instant-messaging their friends over the Internet. Dad's checking out early sports scores in the living room; Mom's watching financial news reports.

As the habits of the American family changed, so too did their viewing patterns. But network evening news on the leading broadcast networks stayed right where it was on the schedule—which meant that a lot of people no longer watched the evening news.

That doesn't mean these people weren't news consumers. The age of empowerment is about choice and convenience. If you want to keep up on network-quality news, you have a dizzying array of options. You can visit any of scores of credible Web news sites throughout the day via a high-speed Internet connection at the office. You can have headlines delivered to a hand-held email device to peruse during your evening commute. You can set a personal video recorder (PVR) such as TiVo to record the network broadcast, then watch it after the kids are tucked into bed. Or you can simply tune to any of the 24-hour national cable TV networks dedicated to news programming.

The advertising business for the last hundred years was based on, indeed cherished, the push model. Advertisers' intrusions were rarely welcome, but they were accepted by consumers as the price they had to pay for essentially free radio and TV programming. The new model that is emerging flips the traditional system on its head. The empowered consumer increasingly has the ability to bypass advertising messages totally. When consumers choose to receive such messages, while shopping for a car, say, they can reach out, via the Internet or a PVR, and pull the message to them. As advertisers lose the ability to invade the home, and consumers' minds, they will be forced to wait for an invitation. This means that they have to learn what kinds of advertising content consumers will actually be willing to seek out and receive.

This switch from the push model to the pull, from intrusion to invitation, is a fundamental transformation for everyone involved in the business of content, whether that content is a 2-hour film, a half-hour sitcom, a radio program, recorded music, an Internet site, or a 30-second advertising message. The end users, rather than the creators and distributors of content, are in control. And that changes all the rules.

These changes have tremendous implications for television advertising and the economic model underlying marketers, ad agencies, and media companies. Since TV is by far the largest, and the most prominent and effective advertising medium, and is still the most cost-efficient way to reach mass audiences, the threat to traditional 30-second commercials (or "spots," in industry parlance) represents a threat to the ability of thousands of companies to market their goods and services.

"We're seeing the fragmentation of markets as invariably people break away into segments based on their personal interests. Talking to people en masse is becoming harder and harder to do," said John Hegarty, a founder and principal of one of the world's most highly regarded creative agencies, London-based Bartle Bogle Hegarty, which among other Madison & Vine–like initiatives formed a record label to create original music that could be used in advertisements and packaged for consumer audiences. "You have to find new avenues to reach them. One of those is to communicate to them in a way that they will invite."

Hegarty, underscoring the powerful hold that TV commercials have on the ad industry, brashly labels TV spots "the most original art form developed in the twentieth century," while reluctantly conceding that they have become less valuable as "the means of delivering them have fragmented."

"We need the ability to get mass impact, because the power of a shared experience is still vital to us. It's a powerful way of getting communications to stick," he said. "People are not fundamentally changing. It's about how do you create that shared experience and do it in a way that captures their imagination?"

At the same time that advertising is being threatened, many sectors of the entertainment business are confronting their own significant challenges. Personal video recorders, the hundreds of channels available on satellite TV and digital cable, and the resulting audience fragmentation are dramatically reshaping the television business. The costs of producing and marketing films are spiraling out of control, damaging Hollywood studios' bottom lines. The music industry has been decimated by online piracy, forcing consolidation among smaller players and the layoffs of thousands of workers.

Despite the urgency created by such upheaval, John Hegarty, like many of his peers, expects there to be strong resistance to change. "The whole model is still being operated on the basis that we're in the 1970s. It will take massive failure for the industry to radically shift, or for someone to succeed brilliantly. People are defending old business models because no one's come up with a new one."

Or have they?

Chapter 2

If It's Broke, Fix It

Now that we have broadly defined the problem, what's the solution? The long-term model, of course, is very much under development; what it will be is still unknowable this early in the change process. But at this point one of the most aggressive responses to the challenges has been for Hollywood and Madison Avenue to explore alliances that integrate content and commerce, that in effect blur the line between traditional entertainment programming and advertising messages. This can take many forms, including:

- *Long-form ads,* so called because they run longer than the usual 30- or 60-second commercials and have an intrinsic entertainment value. BMW Films, a popular series of Internet-distributed mini-movies created by leading Hollywood directors and featuring such stars as Madonna, is the most prominent example, and it has been at the center of a debate on the future of advertising.

- *The integration of product messages* into scripted (sitcoms, soap operas) and unscripted (reality shows, talk shows) TV programming. Coca-Cola's aggressive sponsorship of the hit TV show *American Idol* perhaps best represents what's happened in unscripted programming. On stage, the judges sip Coke out of big cups with the Coca-Cola logo as they listen to the young singers competing for the top prize. Backstage, contestants await the results in a "red room" with a Coca-Cola-red couch, a clock with the soft drink's logo, and, of course, a vending machine. A deal involving the ABC soap opera *All My Children* was an example of product integration in scripted programming. The real-life cosmetics company Revlon paid a fee to be worked into the daytime drama's story line—in a villainous role, no less!—as the fierce competitor to a beauty company controlled by actress Susan Lucci's popular Erica Kane character.
- *Product integration in films.* Placing product in a movie is a practice that has existed since the medium's early days, but now the tie-ins are significantly more extensive. Advertisers can be given input into script development long before filming begins, and they support their presence

in the films with multimillion-dollar advertising campaigns and promotions. The price tag can be huge. Miramax went out to the market asking a record $35 million from automakers interested in cutting a deal to have their vehicle be "a character" in the *Green Hornet* film (the hero's car), even though the film's script hadn't even been written when the studio's marketing departments began making the rounds.

- *Music industry tie-ins.* Music labels are increasingly viewing advertisers as partners in distributing and gaining exposure for new releases, helping to combat the impact of online piracy on CD sales. Respected artists such as the Rolling Stones and Celine Dion are no longer seen as sellouts if they cut deals to create original music or license their existing songs for ads. McDonald's, Mitsubishi, Coca-Cola, Jaguar, and Hewlett-Packard are among the brands that have made such music the centerpiece of their advertising efforts, often resulting in higher sales for the artists who created the songs.
- *Advertiser-funded programming.* Increasingly, advertisers are weighing opportunities to fund the production of TV programs and even films. They do this in part to ensure themselves prime marketing opportunities and shut out rivals and in part to allow them to develop a content environment that they know will be a good fit for their product messages. It also potentially allows them to participate in the success of such

ventures, in some cases through a percentage of profits. For an NBC reality series called *The Restaurant*, about the opening of a high-end eatery in New York City, the media-buying agency Magna Global Entertainment agreed to underwrite most of the production costs and take an ownership position. In exchange, three of its clients—American Express, Coors, and Mitsubishi—were integrated into the plot of the series and got premium commercial positions on the show.

The merging of content and commerce is happening in other media sectors as well. Video-game makers cut deals to integrate products into their game scenarios. Characters in the Sims game have the option of working at a McDonald's restaurant, while the football game Madden NFL incorporates the hard-charging music of bands such as Outkast, Blink 182, and Good Charlotte into its bone-crunching action. Good Charlotte's "The Anthem" was made available on the video game a month before its official release, and Epic Records said that the exposure boosted CD sales significantly (Electronic Arts, maker of the video game, claimed that the song was played more than 500 million times by game players, based on usage statistics).

Even the magazine business, which prided itself for decades on its fierce separation of "church" (editorial) and "state" (business matters), is getting in on the act. Custom-published magazines, titles created solely to advance an advertiser's interest and ensure a friendly editorial environment, have grown slicker and more sophisticated. What once were clearly little more than catalogues are now glossy magazines that hire respected journalists to create full-fledged editorial products that just happen to serve both advertisers and (at least in theory) readers. This segment of the business has exploded in just a few years and now tops $1 billion in revenue. Even traditional magazines have blurred the line; Condé Nast Publications, parent of *Vogue* and *Vanity Fair*, launched a shopping magazine called *Lucky* that doesn't just show readers the latest clothes, makeup, and jewelry but gives them prices and phone numbers so that they can immediately order everything in its pages. The glossy monthly drew howls from more traditional editors because it barely distinguished between advertising and editorial. Yet it was an instant success at attracting readers, quickly reaching a circulation of 800,000. Readers know exactly what they're getting for their money when they pick up the magazine at a newsstand; part of the reason *Lucky* worked was because it was honest about what it was. There was no attempt to deceive the reader while secretly advancing an advertising agenda. *Lucky* proudly was what it was.

New industry sectors are beginning to form around product placement, product integration, and content-commerce alliances. Companies in such areas as commercial production are changing their business models, ad agencies are forming entertainment units, talent agencies are forming brand marketing practices, and a new breed of intermediary is emerging to play matchmaker between marketers and content providers interested in branded entertainment. While there is something of a gold-rush mentality at this point, a land grab, it's beginning to look as if success will result from collaboration more than from competition.

"The biggest hurdle we have to go over, in my opinion, is the integration of the networks, the studios, the ad agencies, the advertisers, the talent agencies, and anybody else that's involved in this space. We must be able to sit down collectively and cooperatively to come up with a solution," said Lee Gabler, co-chairman and partner at Creative Artists Agency (CAA), one of the leading talent agencies in the world. "Right now, the ad agencies are frightened about anybody getting in their space, the networks are in denial, and the advertisers don't have a solution. There is no reason that there have to be winners and losers. The only losers are those who will not participate and will stay on the sidelines and try to continue to do things the way we've done it for the past 30 or 40 years. The winners will be those who recognize there's enough for everybody."

There is much controversy about this new advertising development, particularly centered on the issue of whether the integration of commercial messages into entertainment content will result in blatantly commercial content that will be rejected by audiences. That would create a lose-lose-lose situation for consumers, advertisers, and content providers. The marketplace has already proved that it will reject poor or obvious products, leading, for example, to the cancellation of a pilot program on Time Warner's WB network called *Young Americans* that was funded by Coca-Cola. The show shamelessly plugged Coke as part of its plot lines in a way that turned off viewers (imagine a teen showing his love for a girl he has a crush on by approaching her with an ice-cold bottle of Coke in each hand). Ford seemed to have scored a coup when it got the WB network to name an adventure reality show after its advertising tagline, "No Boundaries." But the show, in which characters set off for adventures in Ford Explorers, was a flop, drawing an average of only about 1 million viewers during its six-episode run. In short, the Hollywood–Madison Avenue intersection will be one of the most important places to be in the next few years for anyone who earns a living in the advertising, marketing, and media industries. Its success or failure at becoming a thriving center of commerce will affect the fortunes of advertisers who rely on mass marketing, will affect the entertainment options of millions of consumers—and will probably affect the economy of the United States and the rest of the world.

"We've gone from an age of interruption to an age of engagement. Before, you could build a model based on interruption because you could get to people and repeat the message over and over again. Now they can avoid us. A large percentage of advertising doesn't work because it doesn't reach people," said the agency executive John Hegarty.

In the future, he said, "The TV commercial will still be fundamentally important. But I can build my message into other forms of communication, which is film, TV programs, even magazines. Tomorrow's products are going to be about entertainment. If it isn't communicated to us in an entertaining way, we're not interested. It's not the end of the commercial if it's entertaining. It's the end of everything if it's not entertaining."

Entertainment, indeed, seems to be the key to invitation. Consumers may read daily newspapers to stay informed and read business-to-business magazines to do their jobs better, but these are more have-to-reads than want-to-reads. They volunteer, however, to spend time being entertained by glossy consumer magazines, CDs, sitcoms, films, or live performances. Even in advertising, the value of entertainment—its ability to draw a viewer's attention—has always been clear. However, one of the ad industry's fiercest ongoing debates centers around whether there is an inherent divide between entertaining and effective advertising. The worst ads are considered to be those that entertain consumers but don't imprint the name of the advertised product, or its benefits and attributes, on the consumers' brains. As with most such debates (nature vs. nurture, for example), it seems that the answer is not either/or but both. The best ads are both entertaining and effective. This seems like a "Duh!" observation, but you wouldn't know it from the passion with which advocates of the two schools of thought are at each other's throats.

As it becomes easier for consumers to ignore and bypass advertising messages, however, it becomes more urgent for advertisers to figure out what will grab their attention. Entertainment, surely, works. A 2002 study of TiVo users revealed that the two types of ads that consumers were least likely to skip were beer commercials and prescription drug advertising. This was not as odd, or as surprising, as it first seemed. Years of witty punch lines, slapstick humor, talking animals, and skimpily clad women (even twins!) have created an expectation that beer ads will be entertaining, conditioning the audience. Pharmaceutical ads were at the other end of the spectrum. They often were creatively lacking but were seen as delivering important information about health and well-being that could perhaps change people's lives for the better (discounting the side effects that are unfortunately catalogued at the end of such ads).

If entertaining ads can grab viewers' attention, imagine the possibilities of embedding the commercial message in entertaining content. It raises the idea of tapping into the bond between content and consumer to a new level, even while putting it at risk. Not only do entertainment tie-ins make the advertising more attractive, they make it impossible to avoid; you can't zap a product placement without zapping the very program you want to watch.

The concept of content-commerce alliances coincided happily with the rise of reality TV (think *Joe Millionaire* or *The Bachelorette*), a genre that seemed ready-made for such tie-ins and can be credited with providing an instant, high-profile platform for such deals. Product integration could never have risen to such prominence so rapidly if TV schedules were still dominated by sitcoms and hour-long dramas— scripted programming with higher aesthetic ideals and a reliance on a long-running future in syndication— rather than by brash reality shows with short shelf lives and an anything-goes sensibility. They make a perfect Petri dish for advertisers who are keen on experimenting with this new format.

Entertainment companies have as much to gain from successful partnerships with marketers. First of all, advertisers no longer view themselves merely as buyers of media time to promote their products. Instead, they often control distribution networks and consumer contact points, which are equally valuable real estate for promoting themselves and other products. When a Disney film ties in with McDonald's, the fast-food chain is able to use its millions of daily contacts with consumers to promote the film—not only through commercials and toy giveaways, but through signs in its restaurants, logos on the cups and bags that customers carry out of stores, buttons on workers' uniforms, even messages on the sides of tractor-trailers that deliver supplies and ingredients.

By providing free products to movies, marketers can lower the cost of producing the film. They also extend the film's marketing budget with their own advertising and promotional dollars. By linking to TV shows, they can offset those shows' production costs as well and continue to provide the revenue stream that keeps stations and networks on the air. For music companies, they can help to promote new releases that otherwise would get scant marketing support. They can also give exposure to new artists by featuring their songs in commercials or distributing their CDs attached to packaging.

There are many tempting opportunities to bring these industries together in a way that benefits all sides and addresses some of the broken elements of their business models. And there are just as many challenges, including the need to prove that such tie-ins actually work, that they provide a sufficient return on investment; the need to present the tie-ins in a way that doesn't offend customers; and the issues of trust between the two sides. Some view the challenges with fear, others with an intoxicating sense of possibility. Among the latter, as noted earlier, is Coca-Cola. Its president became an early and vocal leader of this new movement, and he did it with many entertainment deals, but also with one simple speech.

Chapter 3

Heyer Calling

Steven J. Heyer's keynote speech at *Advertising Age*'s inaugural Madison & Vine conference in Beverly Hills was a call to arms that is still reverberating through the advertising, marketing, and music worlds. Because Heyer is respected as a smart businessman, and—perhaps more important—because he controls a major advertising budget, his words have impact. If he said this was something that the advertising, entertainment, and media industries needed to care about, then they cared about it. And that's exactly what he said. More frightening to listeners was how dismissive he was of any media company, advertising agency, or other marketing vendor who was in denial about the ways in which their worlds were changing, or resistant to that change. Heyer sent a clear signal that Coca-Cola would give its business to anyone who came up with ideas on how it could grow its sales and boost its brand in the new environment. Those that didn't embrace the transformation had no place in that world.

Here is an excerpted version of the speech that may have marked the beginning of a new era:

"At the Coca-Cola Company we're thinking about marketing in a radically different way. Economic and social developments demand a new approach to connecting with audiences, with consumers." Heyer then listed those developments, which he said, included "the erosion of mass markets," "the empowerment of consumers who now have an unrivaled ability to edit and avoid advertising, and to shift dayparts," and "the emergence of an experience-based economy, where cultural production is more important than physical production."

> I am describing a magnitude and urgency of change that isn't evolutionary, it's transformational. And as leaders in consumer packaged goods, Coca-Cola will go first. To accelerate the convergence of Madison & Vine, a convergence of the trinity in brand building—content, media, and marketing.
>
> This is a convergence born of necessity. Economic necessity and marketplace opportunity. We need each other, now more than ever. We need each other to capture people's attention and influence their attitudes and behaviors. The media and marketing executives among us better recognize that corporate marketers will not reflexively turn

to TV advertising when what we [need] is powerful communication and consumer connection.

Even after a record year at the box office, the studio executives among us better recognize that to utilize the same traditional media we do will subject them to the same declines in its efficacy and threaten their results. And maybe even more important, as creators of cultural currency, studios are substantially underleveraging the value of their assets.

The music executives among us better recognize that they are limited by a dissolution of their traditional distribution and business models and by the consolidation of radio, the diminution of MTV's playlist, and by the ever-changing tastes and fleeting loyalties of a consumer with fickle tendencies, an explosion of choice, and a myriad of ways to capture music content.

The television executives among us better recognize [they] are prisoners of media fragmentation and proliferation and the changing media consumption habits of younger generations.

And the [advertising] agency executives, [their] model is in need of a wholesale redefinition. [Their] future will be in working with, not against, content creators. Agencies should be quarterbacking the collaborations. Most undermine them.

So to [Hollywood], we need your content, your storytelling, your influence, your ability to create experiences. We need your ability to help us sell. As you need ours. For ever since Clark

Gable took off his shirt in *It Happened One Night* and sales of men's undershirts plummeted, popular culture, entertainment, has proven its ability to sell products and services, to transform brands and images, to define what's relevant, to facilitate transactions and relationships.

To Madison Avenue, you need our marketing prowess, our reach, our distribution, our day in and day out presence and connection to the lives of our shared audiences around the world.

Together we can be more and do more and make more than any of us can alone. If we do it right. If we do it differently than we've been doing it. If we innovate. If we each do what we're each best at . . . and do it collaboratively.

So how does Madison meet Vine? What's the intersection? It's not the property, the TV show, the movie, the music, or the brand. It's why, where, and how we bring them together. And it is, as ever, about the consumer, all glued together by a powerful idea. It's the insight about people's passions and the connections we create, naturally and uniquely, between them and the equity in our brands. Cultural icons in brand context. Important events tied to important brands.

Our shared challenge isn't just in overcoming the creative and economic tensions that are an inherent part of this convergence of content and commerce. It's about creating more value for the consumer as a way of creating more value for our business and shareholders. It's that simple and that tough. We must create more value for consumers, audiences, and customers, through cooperation, collaboration, and innovation in marketing and communication. Through innovation in the way Madison meets Vine. Through working together to create something for our brands that matters more on Main Street and, ultimately, Wall Street.

For The Coca-Cola Company, creating value around our bottle is the secret formula of Coca-Cola's success. Coca-Cola isn't black water with a little sugar and a lot of fizz any more than one of your movies is celluloid digital bits and bytes, or one of your songs is a random collection of words and notes. Coca-Cola isn't a drink. It's an idea. Like great movies, like great music.

That's a timeless proposition. But we express it in the unique vocabulary of each generation, for what's timeless must also be timely, or it's dated. That's how our products, brands, and businesses stay fresh, relevant, and in demand. It's all about right associations, at the right time with the right idea.

The right associations with the right movies, artists, video games, and events illustrate, enhance, and accelerate the contemporization of core brand values.

But that's no longer enough. So where are we going? Away from [commercials] in pods. Away from broadcast TV as the anchor medium. Away from product placements that are gratuitous because they lack a compelling idea. Because in today's marketing and media environment only the naive and foolish confuse presence with impact. "Presence is easy. Impact is hard."

Where are we headed? We're headed to ideas that bring entertainment value to our brands, and ideas that integrate our brands into entertainment. We're moving to ideas that use celebrities to illustrate, enhance, and extend the values that underpin our brands. We don't want to use talent simply to break through the clutter. Breaking through is a first step, but it's not enough. And, frankly, our brands are bigger than celebrity spokespeople, and borrowed equity only works when you have none of your own.

We will use a diverse array of entertainment assets to break into people's hearts and minds. In that order. For this is the way to their wallets. This much hasn't changed.

We're moving to ideas that elicit emotion and create connections. And this speeds the convergence of Madison and Vine. Because the ideas which have always sat at the heart of the stories you've told and the content you've sold, whether movies or music or television, are no longer just intellectual property. They're emotional capital.

And we will help you create and sell more of it, so that we too can spend it. How? Earlier I'd mentioned the erosion of mass markets. Markets are giving way to networks. In a networked economy, ideas, concepts, and images are the items of real value—you know, marketing. Demand creation and demand fulfillment. And there is no network on earth more powerful than the Coca-

Cola Company—powerful and unbelievably underleveraged. And for the right value proposition and exchange, we are willing to make our network available. This value-for-value exchange is the convergence of Madison and Vine.

The Coca-Cola Company has more impressions than any other company on the planet. You see our brand on cafés, concession booths, and hot dog stands. Our brands light up Times Square and Piccadilly Square, but also neighborhood delis and ballparks. People wear the brand on t-shirts and ball caps. They display it on coolers and beach balls and key chains [and] just about anything you can think of. The Coca-Cola Company in the U.S. spends $1 million on advertising every day that 20 million people see. Thirty million people drink Cokes in exclusive Coca-Cola food-service accounts every day. Twenty million people buy Cokes from vending machines every day. Four million people go see movies sipping on Cokes every day. Twenty-five million people buy our bottles or cans every day. Coke trucks travel over one million miles every day. In total, The Coca-Cola Company benefits from 2 billion-plus brand communication opportunities every day in the U.S. alone.

We have a network of connections no one can match or even approach, that takes us from the biggest events on the planet to the most intimate neighborhood gatherings, from associations with celebrities to partnerships in local sports, film, and music festivals.

It's an impressive list of assets, but that's all it is—a list—unless it's activated and wired in a meaningful way for our brands, our customers, and, of course, our consumer. When it's wired, it's a beautiful thing—a network focused on brand building, capable of delivering a message, a motivation, an idea, a CD, a DVD, a ticket.

Our marketing efforts, our properties and media and celebrity deals, will only produce an adequate return on investment if we use our network of bottlers, customers, promotional partners, properties, and associations to add value beyond the bottle and enrich the lives of our consumers. That's where Madison and Vine ought to converge. But don't yet.

What's going to create the impetus to change? The same things that always do—economic pain and economic opportunity: the commercial time that isn't bought; the movie that can't attract a promotional partner to help it open big; the cable network that can't be launched without seed money from advertisers; the event that can't find sponsors; the song that can't get on the radio; the artist that can't tour.

Intellectually, at least at the macro level, both Madison and Vine are already there. But thought isn't being translated into action just yet, because some are afraid of missing out on important pieces of cultural connection. But in time fear will subside, or the fearful will lose their jobs. And if a new model isn't developed, the old one will simply collapse. People are always saying that this medium or that medium is in decay, declining, going away. No medium goes away; its role changes. That's all. And as media fragmentation continues, and as new choices continue to emerge and technology leaps out ahead of consumers' wishes to change the way they behave, it's incumbent upon us all—advertisers, marketers, creators of content and culture, everyone in this game— to think differently about how we'll connect with consumers in the future.

We view content as a new way to reach and motivate our consumer. It's movies, music, video games that become a component part of our communications strategy and plan. [Entertainment companies] should view us the same way, as a partner and a resource, not just a source of new revenues.

As we move to an experience-based economy, the effective use of relevant and powerful cultural references takes a front seat. Each person's life becomes a commercial market. And any ad agency that thinks a jingle connects like real music or a powerful movie and doesn't collaborate is lost. Most traditional media people think about reach and frequency at a price. And most entertainment people think about Corporate America as a new source of funding for production and a new source of revenue for opening hot and with the power to create a hit. Most marketers think about advertising that packs a punch to reach a target. Imagine if we all thought about the same thing at the same time. Imagine if self-interest took a back seat to mutual interest.

Managing the quality of our consumer relationships should take on the same urgency that controlling the means of production once did. We don't need to own factories, you don't need to own studios. Powerful expression of ideas, not hard assets.

If I'm right about our network and its power, we can help open a movie with our packages, we can popularize and sell new music; we can drive awareness, differentiation and interest. Our goal: to become as critical to your marketing as you are to ours, to leverage our network just like you leverage yours. We're all comfortable with our traditional roles.

Hollywood creates culture, defines what's interesting, hip, and relevant. Madison Avenue interprets brand values and defines the connections to culture in a contemporary and interesting way. Marketers build programs that glue together a multiplicity of relationships to create the reasons why we are entitled to a consumer's loyalty and a premium price.

Those clear-cut definitions fit neatly into a box, defined by uniformity and predictability, which is no longer sustainable in a hyperfragmenting world. If we continue to confine ourselves to those roles, that box is going to become a coffin. The headstone will read: "They didn't try."

All of us in the game, those who make television shows, video games, music, and movies, those who build brands, and those who help connect those brands with consumers through the elements

of popular culture, need to establish enhanced relationships with one another in an effort to deliver
unique experiences to the consumer.

That's a new model for a new era.

P.S.

About nine months after this speech, I checked in with
Heyer to get his sense of what progress had been made
since the speech, to determine how well he believed the
industry had responded to his call for collaboration,
and to see whether his faith in marketing through
entertainment remained strong.

Heyer told me that he remained a strong believer,
but that he has come to realize to an even greater
degree that presence and impact are two different
things, and that while the former is best achieved
through traditional media advertising, the latter comes
from Madison & Vine–type programs.

"Our targets are passionate about a handful of
things—music, sports, visual entertainment, gaming.
Each of those passion points ties to cultural currency,"
he said. "Spots in pods [traditional commercials] are a
great way to capture what's wrong. A message that's
embedded [in content] or enhanced moves you from
presence to impact. That difference between a visual
connection and a visceral connection is money."

Heyer said that the distinction is particularly
important in the soft-drink category, where there is little real difference between Coke and Pepsi, and so marketing plays an important role in creating an aura
around a particular brand. According to consumer

research, while taste is the number one reason people choose a particular soft drink, coming in at a close second in their decision is their belief that the brand fits their lifestyle. That's where marketing comes in.

"We sell an image, not a product. We sell an idea," Heyer said. "It's not about the functional delivery of a functional benefit."

As for the industry's reaction to his speech, Heyer conceded that it was difficult to translate theory into practice, in large part because of a reluctance to dramatically change the way business is done. "Most people are married to traditional business models, and to a degree so are we," he said. In general, he believed that Hollywood—in the form of the movie studios and music labels—was more open to collaboration than Madison Avenue. He attributed that to the entrepreneurial spirit that tends to exist at talent agencies and film and music houses, even those small studios and labels that are part of large corporate media conglomerates. That's because such conglomerates have often been cobbled together via a series of acquisitions of smaller companies with fiercely independent chiefs who insist on maintaining a high level of autonomy as a condition for selling.

"To really get collaboration, you have to work with principals," Heyer said. "Employees are afraid of it. It's not what they get paid to do. Principals recognize that they can become richer and more successful in partnerships."

Large ad agencies and other traditional advertising companies tend to be more bureaucratic, in Heyer's view, and less willing to take risks. They want to lead the process, or even to cut partners out of the loop and provide a one-stop solution. Such territorialism could lead to their downfall, the Coca-Cola chief believes. "It raises a big challenge for large agencies. If they can't retrain people, there'll be a resurgence of small agencies and large agencies will atrophy."

Proof that Heyer believes what he says: In 2003, he pulled Coca-Cola's U.S. advertising account from one of the world's largest ad agencies, McCann-Erickson, and placed it with a small start-up, Berlin Cameron & Partners, whose principals all work directly with their clients.

Chapter 4

Everything Old Is New Again

The broadcasting business is in the midst of a revolution. But advertisers are hanging back, full of questions for which there are few answers: How will the consumer respond? What place will there be for advertising in this new medium? What impact will it have on existing media?

Ad agencies, which are searching for their own role and trying to remain relevant to their clients, are reacting in different ways. Some assign a point person to explore the challenge, others create task forces, and still others do little more than just keep a wary eye on developments. The chief executive of one of the nation's largest ad agencies delivers a speech urging the industry to experiment: "The courage of agencies to change long-established habits and procedures and to get wet all over is, in my opinion, the index to the strength of the advertising agency business in the future."

The time is the present and the subject is the digital revolution, right? Wrong. The time is the late 1940s, and the issue is a new medium called TV. The speaker: advertising legend Leo Burnett, who purchased early TV sets for his top executives and encouraged clients to buy home sets to experience the new medium's power for themselves.

At the time, few people believed that TV was going to be an important medium. Radio played such a dominant role in people's lives immediately after World War II that few believed it could be eclipsed. The combined power of radio, newspapers, and magazines made advertisers reluctant to test the TV waters.

E. F. McDonald Jr., then president of Zenith Radio Corp., told *Advertising Age* in 1945—in perhaps the worst business prediction of the century—that TV "will never make a material bid for the advertiser's dollar."

The similarities between the evolution of the media landscape then and now are striking. Just as the resistance to change sounds familiar, so too does the idea of alliances between the marketing and entertainment industries.

The integration of products into media content is hardly a new phenomenon. Skeptics like to argue that it marks an unimaginative return to the earliest days of television, when sponsors often produced TV shows that were essentially vehicles through which the sponsors could distribute their commercials to an audience that would be entertained and, in theory at least, receptive to an upbeat advertising message promising new and improved products to make their lives easier or happier.

Product placement indeed has its origins in the '50s, but it's more like the 1550s. The colorful British adman John Hegarty gives a speech in which he points out—quoting the research of an Italian university professor and historian named Alessandro Giannatasio—that Venetian painters of that period were known to include in their artwork objects that were unique to, and therefore symbolized the superiority of, their society. The paintings of Paolo Veronese, for example, featured people wearing spectacularly opulent robes and dresses. "Apparently, Veronese's brother was involved in the Venetian fashion business at the time and through Veronese's paintings might have benefited from it," said Hegarty.

Madison & Venice—Who Knew?

Beyond the entertaining notion that there was a form of product placement going on hundreds of years before Milton Berle was born, this anecdote is meaningful in that it underscores the idea that on some level those who are trying to sell goods and services have always looked for ways to integrate their messages into some form of content so that they would gain credibility by becoming part of something that people chose to spend time with.

The Renaissance aside, product placement in a more modern form dates back to the earliest days of radio, when sponsored programming proliferated.

From 1920 to 1922, none of the first 400 radio stations launched in the United States carried advertising, the late Columbia University professor Erik Barnouw wrote in his seminal book *The Sponsor: Notes on Modern Potentates.* Radio programming was created essentially as a way to sell radio sets to the public after the First World War, during which they had been limited to military use. It was AT&T that decided in 1922, controversially and against the wishes of politicians and other critics, to sell radio time to anyone who wanted to buy it to deliver a message to listeners.

The first radio ad came in August of 1922, when the Queensboro Corp., a developer of apartment complexes in Long Island, New York, paid $50 for a 10-minute block of time on New York's WEAF to preach the benefits of suburban living. But in part to blunt the criticism of commercial radio, many stations began instead to allow companies to become the name sponsors of programs or elements within programs, such as the orchestra.

By 1927, NBC's two radio networks were filled with shows such as the *Maxwell House Hour* and *The General Motors Family Party.* Barnouw notes in his book that NBC's first president, Merlin H. Aylseworth, speaking before a congressional committee in 1928, defended program sponsorship as a better option than straightforward advertising: "These clients neither describe their product nor name its price but simply depend on the goodwill that results from their contribution of good programs."

Randall Rothenberg, a journalist and advertising historian, in an essay in *Advertising Age* titled "The Advertising Century," noted that "broadcasting's real birth might . . . accurately be dated to the Postum Co.'s

1926 order that its Philadelphia advertising agency, Young & Rubicam, relocate to New York, the developing center of the broadcast-network business, to handle the account of its Jell-O division. Within eight years, that move bequeathed to the listening public 'The Jack Benny Program,' 'Colgate House Party,' 'General Foods Cooking School' and a smattering of other audience-delighting programs."

The second stage of alliances between advertisers and entertainers soon followed, Rothenberg noted, in the form of celebrity endorsements. Advertisers "borrowed" the popularity of actresses and war heroes to gain instant credibility for their products and services.

A history of Young & Rubicam published in *Advertising Age* expanded on the turning point for the title sponsorship model:

> Some of the aura that surrounds the agency today is rooted in the glory of two of the most remarkable performers of the century—Jack Benny and Fred Allen—whose shows the agency produced every week for General Foods and Bristol-Myers.
>
> Y&R had small hopes in 1934 for Jack Benny, who had been kicking around through two years and three sponsors on NBC's second tier network, NBC Blue. "He was not our first, second or third choice," account executive Louis Brockway later recalled. "But he was available and was the best we could get."
>
> On Oct. 14, 1934, "The Jack Benny Program" went on the air for Jell-O, and his up-to-then sluggish career clicked. By January, Jell-O

had pulled out of its rut and was posting record sales. More important, the Benny program established Y&R as a top radio agency alongside J. Walter Thompson (Bing Crosby and Edgar Bergen/Charlie McCarthy) and Lord & Thomas (Bob Hope). Y&R moved the program to NBC Red in 1936 and stayed with it for the next eight years. When Mr. Benny went to Hollywood in 1936, Y&R went with him, opening its first West Coast office. But the agency's reputation in radio was made within the first 18 months.

Y&R had bought Fred Allen that same year to fill the second half of a one-hour time slot in which Bristol-Myers wanted to sell two products, Ipana toothpaste and a laxative called Sal Hepatica. It was ad dogma at the time that each sponsor needed consistent identification with a single program. Accordingly, Y&R created two shows: a music format for Ipana and the Allen show for Sal Hepatica. When the music show tanked and Allen took off, though, Bristol-Myers complained that Ipana was getting the brush.

Y&R responded with a profound nugget of common sense: expand Allen to a full hour under a dual sponsorship. The result was "Town Hall Tonight" and the first provisional steps toward broadcasting's ultimate destiny: participating sponsorship.

Some popular personalities and formats were unable to make the transition from radio to television, but the product placement and title sponsorship models translated seamlessly to the new medium. Advertisers had considerable sway because radio and TV were "free" media as far as consumers were concerned, beyond the purchase price of a radio or TV set. For broadcasters, advertising was the sole source of revenue and profits. That fact was hammered home repeatedly to viewers, not only in the commercials that interrupted the programming, but during the programming itself. Game show hosts would stop in the middle of a show to do a live commercial for their presenting sponsors.

Procter & Gamble managed to create and essentially name a genre of programming. Its daytime "soap operas" were an effective tool for gathering millions of women around the TV set at the same time so that the maker of Tide and Ivory could pitch its laundry detergents and bath soaps. The first radio soap opera, *Oxydol's Own Ma Perkins*, debuted in 1933. In the 1940s, P&G funded production of soaps such as *As the World Turns,* which were platforms for promoting its products—not through the story lines, but through commercial interruptions. The soap operas were the perfect platforms for P&G's spots.

"Throughout the whole middle part of this century, the soap opera was a tremendous vehicle with tremendous reach," former P&G marketing chief Bob Wehling told *Advertising Age* in 1999. "It was the principal vehicle used to launch Tide, Crest and a whole host of other brands."

Barnouw notes in *The Sponsor* that paid product placements also evolved during TV's earliest days: "Drama writers and directors were advised that if they could make potato chips a part of any happy party scene, a $100 check would be forthcoming from a publicity agent—who had, in fact, a long list of products that could earn similar payoffs."

There were a number of factors involved in the transition from title and single sponsorship to the multisponsor format that prevails today. Early shows were presented live from New York. As shows began to be shot on film in Hollywood studios, however, the cost of producing them increased greatly. Advertisers no longer wanted to bear the entire cost burden of a show. Allowing multiple sponsors was a way to lessen the risk and spread the costs. It also got the advertisers out of the business of owning programming, which clearly wasn't their core business, and put networks back in charge of their own schedules and offerings. Studios began to fund production of shows at a loss for their first run on network TV, in anticipation of a strong aftermarket in syndication and international markets. Networks paid a fee to air the programs and made their money on ad sales.

There was strong proof as well that TV commercials worked when it came to moving products off shelves. Every student of advertising knows the story of Hazel Bishop lipsticks, one of the earliest companies to experiment with TV advertising. Its sales soared hundredfold after just 2 years of using the medium to promote its product.

The quiz show scandals of 1959 also hastened the demise of single sponsorships. Revlon—which had turned to TV advertising to regain the market leadership it had lost to Hazel Bishop—was the presenting sponsor of *The $64,000 Question*, which was found to have given answers to favored contestants in advance to maintain the program's popularity. To restore their credibility with viewers, TV networks took back control from the sponsors, something they had been itching to do anyway. ("Network leaders had long chafed over the degree of control they had yielded, in early broadcasting history, to agencies and sponsors," Barnouw wrote in *The Sponsor*.)

Today, with production costs spiraling out of control and the aftermarket becoming less lucrative, show owners are looking for new sources of funding, and once again advertisers are being eyed for that role. One form this is taking, of course, is product placement and sponsored segments of programs. But the idea of advertisers owning stakes in shows in exchange for favorable advertising positions, category exclusivity, and script integration is also being toyed with. Everything old is new again.

Chapter 5

A VCR on Steroids

In the fall of 2002, AdAge.com published an eye-catching headline: "More U.S. homes have outhouses than TiVos." It was a fact; at the time, TiVo had about half a million subscribers, some 150,000 fewer than the number of homes that lacked indoor plumbing.

While this was certainly an interesting bit of trivia, the figures were almost beside the point. The story was about the challenge one company faced in growing its subscriber base, but it made clear that whether or not TiVo succeeded in reaching a mass market, this technology, the digital video recorder, was "on its way to mainstream adoption." The point was soon moot in any case—one year to the day after the "outhouse" headline appeared, TiVo announced that it had reached the 1 million mark in subscribers. I didn't double check, but it's a safe bet that the number of outhouses remained relatively static over that same period.

It didn't seem to matter, though, that the statistic, while fun, was essentially misleading. All over the TV and advertising industries, you began to hear the "outhouse" line quoted, mostly by old-school executives who were comfortable with the status quo and felt threatened by the new technology. They latched onto the numbers like a lifeline, brandishing them as proof that the DVR threat had been overstated.

They couldn't have been more wrong.

TiVo is a relatively small company with a funny name, tucked away in northern California. It pulled in only about $100 million in revenue in its most recent fiscal year. It wasn't in business a decade ago, and it may not be in business a decade from now.

Yet the San Jose, California, software maker represents perhaps the biggest threat ever faced by the multibillion-dollar giants that rule the television industry and the mass marketers that saturate the airwaves with their sales pitches. While some people still scoff at TiVo's size and strategy, it's become clear that what TiVo offers—a technology that puts viewers in charge of their TV sets and enables them to schedule their own programming and obliterate unwanted advertising messages—is unstoppable. Yet TiVo's blessing and curse was that it had by then become almost a generic name for DVRs (think Q-Tips and cotton swabs, Kleenex and facial tissues), and its ups and downs were mistaken for indicators of the future of its segment. Tellingly, TiVo became a verb; you didn't record a TV show, you "TiVoed" it. If people weren't buying the branded boxes faster than consumer electronics manufacturers could make them, some near-sighted executives believed that this meant that DVRs were going nowhere, that they were a technology in search of a market. What they missed, somehow, was the inevitability of the functionality, the seeming surety that within a few years DVRs would not only be available through stand-alone set-top boxes but would be embedded in cable boxes, satellite TV receivers, even TV sets. They also didn't see the implications of how quickly early adopters had embraced the control that DVRs gave them, how rapidly they had evolved into a new species: the empowered viewers who didn't need network programmers—because they were their own network programmers.

According to a study by the Yankee Group, digital video recorders such as TiVo will be in 20 percent of U.S. households by the year 2007, putting an estimated $5.5 billion in advertising revenue at risk by then. (The figures are based on the assumption that such households will watch the majority of their programming off the hard drive on a time-shifted basis and will skip over about 80 percent of the advertising, estimates that were based on the habits of early DVR adopters.) So seriously are those numbers taken that the chief executive of one of the world's largest advertising holding companies—which derives more than half its revenue and profit from media advertising—confided to me that he had set 2007 as a personal deadline for reinventing the company to tap new sources of revenue before it and his job become obsolete.

There are those who believe that DVRs are a threat to the TV business, but that's probably not true. They are sure to dramatically reshape television and advertising, but they will destroy only those who lash themselves to the doomed current business model and resist change.

What exactly do DVRs do? They've been called VCRs on steroids, but they are really much more of a leap forward than that, just as DVDs are vastly superior to VHS tapes. DVRs offer far more choice and convenience. They are essentially digital storage devices that allow viewers, at the touch of a button, to record TV programs on a hard drive and watch them whenever they want. There's no need to program a VCR or look for a blank tape or label the show. DVRs have their own on-screen program guides, and simply by pushing a button or two users can instruct the machine to record a single episode of a show or a full season. The searches can get much more specific as well. Want your DVR to record any Paul Newman movies that come on and store them on your private Paul Newman network? No problem. Want to create a channel for your kids featuring only programs that you've approved? Simple. "There are many parents that actually create networks for their kids. They're allowed to watch anything they want on TiVo," said entertainment marketing consultant Mitch Kanner. "To them it's a network. Their channel is TiVo. Anything that's on there, they can watch. What a great parental tool." And once they sit down to watch a show on DVR, the viewers have full control over the programming. They can pause it, fast-forward, reverse, and so forth.

An even more practical use of the DVR is to pause a broadcast show. Have to take a phone call in the middle of your favorite medical drama? No problem. Just hit the pause button and the DVR begins recording. After the call, and perhaps even after a visit to the bathroom and the fridge, you can pick up the show exactly where you left off. The simplest way to catch up to the live show if you don't want to miss the start of the next program? Fast-forward—gasp!—through the commercials. My kids go to bed at 9 on school nights, and by the time I've read them a story and settled them down, it's close to 9:30. So each Wednesday I set my DVR to record NBC's White House drama *The West Wing*, which begins at 9 p.m. After the kids are asleep, I begin watching the show off the hard drive. By skipping commercials (why in the world wouldn't you?), I make up most of the time and finish watching the program just a few minutes later than those people who have been watching it "live."

It was inevitable that this would happen to TV. The rise of the Internet gave consumers unprecedented control over information and entertainment and exposed the unacceptable absurdity of network TV schedules that couldn't be adjusted to suit individual lives. The Internet let users find what they wanted when they wanted it—headlines, stock prices, sports scores, weather forecasts from the city they were about to travel to. Yet when these same people got home from work, they still had to wait for the 11 p.m. local newscast to get the five-day forecast or seek out the Weather Channel and even then wait for it to stop telling you the temperature in Tel Aviv and Frankfurt and get around to your home town. And if you loved *Late Night with David Letterman*'s nightly Top 10 countdown, but you wanted to be asleep by a decent hour because you had an appointment in the morning, you were out of luck. Maybe one of your coworkers would remember a couple of the wittier lines and share them over coffee in the office.

TiVo changed all that.

TiVo and its ilk did a poor job of marketing early on, and it was difficult to explain to nonusers what the big deal was. (The exception was a brilliant and hilarious early TiVo commercial that didn't demonstrate the product's capabilities but made vividly clear how intoxicating empowerment can be. The ad starred "Earl," a man who, after getting a TiVo, always wants to get his own way, whether this means driving against traffic or picking out an unusual pet—"I don't want a puppy; I want the tiger," he says at one point.) The passion the technology evoked in converts was so strong that they became an evangelical, volunteer word-of-mouth sales force for the product. Once you believed, you believed. And TiVo's usage statistics backed up the idea that the device had a dramatic impact on viewing habits. "People who couldn't program a VCR, they can't live without TiVo," one devotee told me.

TiVo users watch the majority of their TV off the hard drive, tending to view only sports, reality, and news (nonscripted) programming in real time, largely because of its immediacy and water-cooler value. And when they watch shows they've recorded, they don't watch ads.

A CNW Marketing Research study found that DVR users skipped commercials a stunning 72.3 percent of the time. That compared to 45 percent who said they didn't watch commercials while watching live TV and just 15.6 percent who said they skip commercials on videotapes. Certain categories, including fast food, credit cards, and TV network promotions, were bypassed 90 percent of the time by DVR users. Imagine being a marketing executive in one of those industries and projecting those figures out to a point where DVRs are in tens of millions of homes. It's too frightening to consider. (As for the 45 percent who said they didn't watch commercials during live TV broadcasts, it came as no surprise to TV ad buyers or sellers. It's been the industry's dirty little secret for years that many people change channels or walk away from the set during commercial breaks. But while those defections can be easily overlooked as part of the cost of doing business, the DVR viewership losses can't be ignored. The data are indisputable.)

The TV industry had problems long before DVRs. In the 1950 broadcast season, *Texaco Star Theater* on NBC averaged a 62 rating and an 81 share, authors Ed Keller and Jon Berry note in their book about the power of word of mouth, *The Influentials* (The Free Press, 2003). That means that 62 percent of all the TV sets in the United States and an incredible 81 percent of those sets that were turned on at the time were tuned in to the show. By comparison, ABC's 1999 hit *Who Wants to be a Millionaire?* averaged an 18.6 rating and a 29 share.

"Back in the days when 'The Beverly Hillbillies' could get a 50 or better share of the audience watching television on any given night, getting your message across to Americans was relatively easy," the authors wrote. "Television literally made brands. Revlon's sales jumped 54% in 1955, the year it began sponsoring 'The $64,000 Question' on CBS."

Broadcast TV was ruled by three networks in the 1950s and 1960s, and it became the dominant advertising medium because of its unprecedented reach and power. It gave marketers the ability to deliver their messages simultaneously to tens of millions of consumers and hammer them home repetitively. No other medium could offer anything close. TV also had the advantage of having a finite and fleeting advertising inventory. Once all the ad time in a given evening was sold, there was no room for more. Commercial slots were like airplane seats, and when demand was high, the networks could jack up prices just as the airlines do. Magazines, by comparison, have virtually unlimited advertising inventory. If more advertisers want to buy space, the publisher simply adds more pages. A magazine can be as fat, or as thin, as the publisher chooses to make it, giving it no supply-side leverage.

The 1970s and 1980s saw the rise of cable TV from a sort of super-antenna enabling people in rural areas to get better reception to a programming medium that was able to serve diverse, often narrow, audience slices with shows that catered to their interests—in movies, cooking, shopping, soap operas, even the weather.

Consumers and advertisers went from having three over-the-air channel choices to a dozen, then 50, then 80. Today, subscribers to cable and digital TV have hundreds of options on the dial and rely on on-screen interactive programming guides for listings, as these can no longer be easily stuffed into the print edition of the digest-size magazine *TV Guide* or summarized on a page in the local newspaper. Cable also had something else that broadcast didn't—it had revenue from subscribers as well as advertisers, and that changed the economic model for cable networks, lessening their dependency on the almighty ad dollar.

For a long time cable amounted to little more than a gnat to the broadcast elephants, but it grew over time, fragmenting audiences and eating into the Big Four (Fox had by now become a factor) networks' share of viewers and ad dollars. Even as cable grew, though, the networks were able to convince advertisers that their audience declines somehow made them even more valuable, since they were the last places left where large numbers of people could be reached at once with an ad message. So even as audiences shrank, the broadcasters hiked commercial rates and used their fixed inventory to force advertisers to pay up or risk being shut out. It was laughably absurd, and yet advertisers paid. They feared not being able to market their products through the medium or being forced to justify paying a much higher price than others were paying.

Each spring, buyers and sellers of TV commercial time engage in a long-standing, increasingly foolish ritual known as the prime-time upfront, where commercial time is sold months in advance of the coming fall season. Since the networks control the supply and decide what percentage of their new-season commercial inventory—usually 70 to 80 percent—they will put up for sale during this period, they effectively create artificial demand. Advertisers who wait until the fall season to buy the remaining time usually pay a hefty premium and miss out on the audience guarantees that upfront buyers are offered, creating an incentive for them to stick with a way of doing business that they are aware makes absolutely no sense.

Still, the networks' ability to perpetuate this model in the face of evidence that it is of no advantage to the people who should have the clout and say-so, the advertisers, is one of the great mysteries of the modern age. Every year, the grumbling grows a little louder as advertisers question the effectiveness and efficiency of their broadcast buys, yet the networks continue to hit new revenue heights. In 2003, the upfront reached a record $9.3 billion. Still, many believe that the collapse of this market is inevitable and less than a decade away. In fact, the 2003 fall TV season began as a dismal failure, with no obvious network hits and big audience declines, particularly among the young males so coveted by advertisers.

More and more questions are being raised about the effectiveness and value of network television, and more advertisers are promising to begin to seriously explore alternatives. A fall 2003 survey done for the Association of National Advertisers' annual meeting found that marketers consider network TV to be the medium that does the worst job of proving return on investments. Bill Lamar Jr., head of U.S. marketing for McDonald's, gave a keynote speech at the annual American Association of Advertising Agencies conference in spring 2003, in which he warned that the fast-food chain planned to spend less money on TV advertising and to invest more in digital media. "The days of spending hundreds of millions of dollars on TV advertising are over," he said. "Reaching consumers is no longer TV-driven. We must have insights that connect us to individual consumers at the right time and in a place where that consumer is most receptive to our message." He cited the chain's deal with The Sims online game as an example.

Martin Yudkovitz, a former NBC executive who is now president and chief operating officer of TiVo, is one of those who believe that the shell game has about run its course. He contends that the advertising business model that relies on 30-second broadcast prime-time TV commercials as its primary tool is already broken. Like many others, he notes that even before DVRs, as many as four in ten viewers walked away from the set during commercial breaks to visit the refrigerator or the bathroom or to make a phone call. Remote controls made it easier for even those who remained on the couch to avoid advertising by flipping channels during commercial breaks.

So as the cost of buying commercials on broadcast networks rose, audiences were splintering into smaller groups. "The value that advertisers were receiving was deteriorating," Yudkovitz said.

Everyone knew that a great deal of the $60 billion spent on TV advertising was wasted on audience members that the advertisers just didn't even want to reach, let alone the 40 percent that weren't watching. There was no accountability, there was no strong measurement of commercial watching, there was no efficiency.

Advertisers were screaming, saying, "You invented this medium, you invented this business model where we entertain and then we ambush with an ad, and nothing has changed in 50 years." What industry has gotten away with not serving its customers with any additional value for 50 years and survived? It was decaying, it was broken, it was already in serious trouble. TiVo exacerbated the problem. But TiVo didn't create the problem.

While Yudkovitz may have an agenda in taking this position, he is far from alone in his viewpoint. Lee Gabler, a soft- but blunt-spoken co-chairman and partner of Hollywood talent agency Creative Artists Agency who oversees the television and marketing divisions, shares Yudkovitz's view; he even believes that the progression is a natural one and not necessarily bad for the business.

"Advertisers, networks and studios have been doing the same thing for years and it's time for change. The model is just not as effective as it was when it was first developed," Gabler said. Noting that automobiles are improved almost annually, he added, "The advertising business has not matured in the past 30 or 40 years. I wouldn't blame the current need for change on TiVo. It's an evolutionary process that has stagnated because advertisers and networks have been slow to recognize and adapt to changes in the consumer marketplace. We all now need to find a new solution."

The TV networks and their advertisers are trying to do exactly that.

Chapter 6

Dial It Up

Imagine paying $12,000 to watch a commercial. OK, an underwear commercial. OK, a live, hour-long underwear commercial in which the garments are worn by the world's sexiest models. Starts to make a little more sense, perhaps. But still, $12,000?

That, according to *The Wall Street Journal*, was the market value of a ticket to attend the 2003 Victoria's Secret Holiday Fashion Show in New York City, which featured lingerie-clad runway models wearing angels' wings; performances by Sting, Mary J. Blige, and Eve; and an after-show party at which Donald Trump rubbed elbows with P. Diddy. But while the annual star-studded event is a hot ticket, this isn't really what the show is about. The runway show is filmed for a broadcast that has pulled in decent ratings for the TV networks, including ABC and CBS, on which it has appeared (although those ratings seem to dip a bit more each year). It attracts young men, an elusive but much-desired advertising target, and it draws millions of dollars in free publicity, including that *Wall Street Journal* story, which appeared on the business bible's front page along with a full-body, full-color shot of model Gisele Bündchen in a racy angel-wing getup. Even the controversies that surround the show—conservative watchdog groups complain loudly each year about its overt sexuality and threaten boycotts—mostly result in added exposure. At the show itself, in 2003, more than 100 newspaper photographers and TV camera operators were crammed onto a platform that capped the runway.

No matter what bells and whistles are wrapped around it, though, the fashion show ultimately is what it is: an hour-long commercial for a retail chain. It's also a fairly brilliant example of a melding of entertainment and advertising. Viewers know exactly what they're in for when they watch it, but they consider the trade-off (getting to stare at beautiful women in their scanties in exchange for being bombarded with Victoria's Secret logos and branding messages) to be worth it. The entertainment value is there. Victoria's Secret seems to believe that the show is worth the investment, although the company's sales in 2003 were up only slightly compared to the previous year.

The Victoria's Secret show is just one of many ways in which entertainment-advertiser alliances are being brought to the small screen. The modern return of product integration in programming can be traced to the rise, starting in 2000, of a new form of programming, largely imported from the United Kingdom, known as "reality television." These unscripted shows, featuring real-life people in interesting situations, are a lot cheaper to produce than scripted sitcoms and dramas, but they don't have an afterlife in syndication. To make more money on them in first-run television, therefore, the idea of charging sponsors to be a part of the programs themselves was hatched.

The ABC game show *Who Wants to Be a Millionaire?* and the CBS program *Survivor,* in which groups of people are stranded on deserted islands and the like, compete for rewards, and vote one another off the show, are considered pioneers in this new/old form of product placement.

On *Millionaire,* hosted by Regis Philbin, contestants were given three so-called lifelines, opportunities to reach out to others in the audience for help in narrowing down a list of possible answers to trivia questions. AT&T sponsored one lifeline that allowed the contestant to telephone a friend or family member for help.

Survivor's plugs were even more blatant, with sponsors' products being used as rewards in the program. The winner of a particular contest might be given a Domino's pizza after subsisting on berries and insects for several days, or a six-pack of cold beer after a day of grueling physical activity in the sun. Viewers didn't seem to mind the product placements in the reality shows, in part because the products seemed to fit well with the programs and in part because their expectations for these shows was already somewhat lowered by the shows' sensationalistic formats.

"The effectiveness of what *Survivor* did was phenomenal," said CBS Chairman-CEO Leslie Moonves.

"It far surpassed what you would get from a 30-second spot, or even five 30-second spots, to have somebody say, 'Oh, my God, a Dorito chip,' as if it were manna from heaven or, 'Oh, my God, I get to drink a Budweiser. I haven't had alcohol in four weeks. This beer tastes so good.' I think that's better than having three guys [in a commercial] sitting in a bar watching a football game saying, 'Look at this Budweiser.' The seeds are planted, clearly, for the future."

In addition to the added credibility for a brand of being part of the script, product placements have another advantage: They can't be zapped by the viewer unless the viewer is leaving the show. Suddenly, such placements were raised to a new level: They were seen by some as a possible savior for the television model. As the DVR threat grew larger, bringing predictions of the death of the 30-second commercial, product integration began to be seen as a life preserver. At the same time, reality TV exploded in popularity, drawing big audiences that were interested in voyeurism, in seeing others humiliated or at least humbled. TV schedules became filled with such fare—shows in which gaggles of attractive young women vied for the attentions of a rich bachelor, or a poor bachelor pretending to be rich, or in which groups of people were forced to live together in seclusion for a month, an experiment in how much they could get on one another's nerves before someone's sanity snapped.

The cable network Bravo, partly owned by NBC, produced a surprise hit with *Queer Eye for the Straight Guy*, a show in which a team of five gay men took on the task of making over a style-challenged straight man by offering home decorating tips, shopping for a new wardrobe, and visiting salons. Retailers, including the home store Pier 1 Imports, eagerly signed on with the show. The "Fab Five" and their straight guy were often shown on shopping trips, with store signs visible as they walked in and shopping bag logos cramming the camera on the way out. ABC made a similar deal for a reality special called "Extreme Makeover: Home Edition," which aired in December 2003. It signed a deal to showcase Sears products, including tools, appliances, and delivery trucks, in the show, which focused on a home rehabilitation.

Matti Leshem is one of the more high-profile producers of reality television. A former partner of British producer Michael Davies, who introduced *Who Wants to Be a Millionaire?* to U.S. audiences, Leshem in 2003 set up his own production company, Protagonist, with Pepsi-Cola Company as his first client. Leshem earlier had produced a reality series for Pepsi on the WB network, *Play for a Billion*, in which contestants competed for the chance to win a $1 billion grand prize.

Brand integration will be a cornerstone of Leshem's production company, yet he remains a skeptic, being unconvinced that this is the ultimate solution and being certain that many people will do a poor job of it, increasing viewers' resistance. "You have to be wary. We're at the inception of this movement," Leshem said. "This is the sweet spot that lies between the brand, advertising, marketing, and television production. But you will never get a rating unless you get the audience to care. You have to have an emotional connection with the viewers."

One of Leshem's first and more ambitious attempts at marrying programming and marketing never got off the ground. Leshem and Davies had planned to create a TV show, *Live from Tomorrow*, that would have no commercial interruptions, but instead would rely solely on brand integration. The plan was to sign two major sponsors at $4.1 million apiece and four minor sponsors at $1.6 million each for the first six episodes, which would cost less than $1 million each to produce.

Live from Tomorrow planned to make the sponsors' brands an essential part of the program, which was to be a sort of high-tech variety show. One planned segment would have been a scavenger hunt in which contestants would roam the country in sport-utility vehicles, using cell phones to collect clues and digital cameras to photograph landmarks and the like. The vehicles, phones, and cameras, of course, would be products made by the show's sponsors.

Leshem doesn't believe there will be much consumer resistance to such tie-ins. "I look at it from a very populist point of view. We live in a culture of brands. It's the way we connect to the world."

Industry resistance is another story. "Ad agencies broke down into two camps: those that felt threatened and those that got what we were doing and told their clients to get in," Leshem said. Although *Live from Tomorrow* never made it to the air, it did introduce Leshem to Pepsi, which had been the first sponsor to sign on, and led ultimately to the creation of the *Play for a Billion* show.

A big believer in the reality genre as a platform for brand alliances, Leshem is surprisingly resistant to the migration of the concept to scripted programming such as sitcoms and hour-long network dramas. In that sense, he is something of a purist, seeing scripted programming as a more sacred form that could ruin its bond with audiences by introducing branded content.

"It doesn't belong in scripted programming. Scripted programming is like a novel or a short story. It's an immersive and passive experience, and it shouldn't be fucked with," Leshem said.

The issue of whether and when product integration will leap from reality to scripted programming is in fact one of the biggest issues facing TV, and the outcome will affect the networks, producers, ad sales forces, and even the actors and actresses who populate these shows. While some share Leshem's view that scripted programming is untouchable, others believe it is inevitable that brands will play a bigger role in sitcoms and dramas as PVR penetration reaches critical mass. There have already been some attempts, for example, the inclusion of Revlon in the plot lines of the daytime soap opera *All My Children.*

It helps that one of the more vocal proponents of brand tie-ins in scripted material is one of TV's most powerful executives and one of the people responsible for introducing the concept to reality programming.

CBS's Moonves has obviously given the issue a lot of thought. The first time I sat with him formally to discuss the topic, he began talking before I could ask a single question, and his comments neatly encompassed

the major issues facing the networks and their advertisers and viewers.

Moonves predicted that PVRs would hit critical
mass around 2006 and at that point would become "a
significant problem" for the networks.

> Obviously if you're not aware of them,
> your head is in the sand, and if you're not
> preparing for the future, you're being
> pretty dumb about it. If you have a way to
> block out my commercials, I've got to find
> different ways of getting the advertiser's
> message to you. *Survivor*—(a CBS
> show)—started it in this round by really
> incorporating product into the show. It's
> obviously a lot easier to do with a reality
> show than with a scripted program, al-
> though you're going to see that in the fu-
> ture. As we go down the road, you're
> going to see it incorporated into drama
> and comedy.

Moonves said that the key will be breaking down
the resistance of writers, directors, and actors. "The creative people are finally coming around to [accepting
that] it's not sacrilegious that *Everybody Loves Ray-
mond* might have a can of Coke on the table, that it's
not destroying their artistic integrity to incorporate
this, because it's a fact of life."

Helping to overcome their concerns is the economics of producing a network TV program. Deals
with marketers can help to offset production costs.

With *Survivor* we were basically at break-
even that first summer no matter what because of product placements. If [a
scripted-programming producer] comes to
us and says, "Look, I would rather incorporate some product placements within my
new show than have my license fee cut; I'd
rather have that extra $100,000 a week to
put on the screen than have you tell me I
can only do the show for this amount," it's
a fair trade-off for me. Everybody's getting
ready for it, and I think you're going to see
it enter into more and more programs.

Moonves said that scripted programs will have to
make sure that product placements are fairly subtle and
that they enhance rather than interfere with the plot,
which he doesn't think will be too difficult to pull off.

We have sat down with car companies.
Let's say I'm [talking about] *CSI Miami* [a
CBS crime drama]. What if [lead actor]
David Caruso is driving a Buick or a Cadil-
lac, and a couple of times during the hour
you do a scene with him leaning on the car
with the logo right next to him, something
like that where you try not to intrude but
it's there. I don't think it's a bad thing, and
I don't think that's intrusive.

Family sitcoms are a particularly juicy target, in
Moonves's view. Many scenes take place in kitchens, for

example, which can easily be stocked with real-life brands: cola bottles, cereal boxes, canned soups, and dishwashing detergent, among others.

Those deals will eventually be sold jointly, he believes, by the network's sales force and the show's producers. Although he expects some sitcom actors to "want a piece of the action," he doesn't think they will be paid based on product placement deals. There are also bound to be conflicts between products integrated into shows and rival brands endorsed by the star of a show, but Moonves noted that the network has the right to approve or deny endorsement opportunities for the stars of its shows.

While their bosses may believe in product integration, network ad sales executives have been slower to embrace it. Critics suggest that this is because they are used to a more comfortable way of doing business that revolves around selling 30-second commercial interruptions and they are threatened by integration deals, unsure of how to price or measure them or how to deal with competitive issues. If Campbell Soup cuts a deal to appear in a sitcom, you can't turn around and sell a commercial unit in the program to Progresso. When the media-buying giant Mindshare reached an agreement to give its clients a first shot at product integration deals on ABC TV shows, it was the network's chief programmer who hammered out the deal, not the head of ad sales.

A veteran of the network TV business who asked not to be identified said that it will take external pressure from advertisers and agencies as well as internal pressure from upper management to get sales forces to change the cozy and ingrained ways they do business, which include long expense-account lunches and golf outings with favored clients, with whom they've had relationships for decades in some cases.

"Network sales guys have it all figured out now. Just don't screw up their lives," the executive said. "They don't need the new equation. They need their golf games, they need to retire in 5 years, and they've got it nailed. So there is great resistance to it. But the impetus is coming from the advertisers' clients themselves, who are pounding on their agencies for more accountability, more value. That will slowly filter through, and this will be done."

Another long-time observer of the television industry seconded that analysis. "In my experience, I have found that the network salespeople are paranoid about anybody having any conversation that has anything to do with anything other than 'I'll see you in May [for the upfront selling period] and we'll talk about ad spots.' Anything creative you can forget about."

But network executives tend to dismiss such generalizations about their sales forces.

"The old timers absolutely will" resist change, Moonves conceded, but "they're not going to be around to have to figure it out." The younger generation that is rising through the ranks, he said, grew up with digital technologies and are eager to have a say in redefining the business. "We're finding little resistance from our salespeople. They were very gung-ho about getting out there and selling in a different way, about how to make this work. They're not stupid. A guy who's

30 years old and selling, he's going to be around for 30 more years. He knows this is coming."

Another model that some observers expect to emerge is to have sponsors take equity positions in shows, to become owners. That could increase the risk for the sponsor, but it also increases the potential upside if the show is a success. And it gives advertisers a chance to have more of a say in how their products are written into scripts. That happened with *The Restaurant* on NBC, in which media agency Magna Global took an ownership position in exchange for getting its clients exposure on the series. The head of Magna Global's entertainment unit even appeared in the credits as an executive producer of the show.

"It's a question of whether or not the sponsor can get more actively involved in the creation of programming earlier in the process, in concert with the network," said Bruce Redditt, who runs the entertainment assets of ad agency giant Omnicom Group. He said that there are various financing models that could emerge. As one example, he cited Pepsi, which underwrote the production costs of six hour-long music specials in the summer of 2003, and in exchange had its brand linked with "very hot, edgy, and hip music talent."

"They were able to affect the way that programming was developed. You're going to see more of that," said Redditt.

> You could see a client owning a block of time on a network. We've had some discussions with various people in Hollywood around such an idea, of owning a Saturday

night block of time in which it would be family-friendly, kid-friendly programming to bring families back to the network. There are other things where you're just absolutely developing programming from scratch. You have an idea that resonates with a particular brand; the brand surrounds it, sponsors it, underwrites it; it becomes a living, breathing part of the brand. In most cases, advertisers aren't looking to get in the back end for the profit, they're looking to influence the script. These clients are not in the entertainment business, they're in the brand business of selling. On the other hand, [profit] participation is a nice thing if there is that opportunity.

Chapter 7

TiVo's Future

One of the most interesting things about what could arguably be called the "TiVo Revolution" is that TiVo may not be around to witness its outcome.

The question isn't whether DVRs will reach critical mass. They will, and this will transform the advertising and media landscapes. The question is whether TiVo will be a leading DVR player when that happens. Its future success could depend on an Intel-like strategy—its ability to position itself as a branded ingredient that enhances another product (in this case, not the guts of personal computers but those of cable set-top boxes).

Martin Yudkovitz was a long-time NBC executive who became president of TiVo in April 2003, an insider who went over to what some network bigwigs still viewed as the enemy camp. That said, NBC had been an early investor in TiVo, to the tune of around $5 million. This was in part to hedge its bets (at the time, NBC had a small stake in about 60 emerging-media technologies) and in part to help influence the technology's development—to have a say, for example, in whether TiVo would allow users to skip entire ads or merely to blurrily fast-forward through them. For some reason this became an important distinction among advertising executives, who believed that they still had some chance of making a branding impression in a speeded-up blur, but that they lost even that opportunity when users could jump forward in 30-second leaps as they could with Replay TV, a smaller rival to TiVo. They succeeded in keeping a 30-second skip button off the TiVo remote.

If Yudkovitz had one significant advantage in joining TiVo from the outside, it was that he understood instinctively what the company's founders— engineers, not marketing experts—hadn't grasped: The company could no longer rely solely on stand-alone DVRs (think of a high-tech VCR connected to the TV), a market it dominated with about an 80 percent share. To remain a leading player, the software marketer had to grow its satellite TV base and convince the cable industry that "TiVo inside" the cable box could help cable systems gain and retain subscribers and wring more revenue from them. No easy task that. He also focused on premium services that allowed TiVo to stand for more than basic DVR functionality, since cable companies were beginning to offer that to their subscribers on their own. In 2003, Time Warner Cable began to offer DVR functionality to digital-cable subscribers for $10 a month, and the company claimed to have several hundred thousand subscribers just a few months after it began peddling the devices.

"The new technology provides the tools to provide new value to the advertising. And if you provide this new value, these tools can more than offset the loss of value from the technology," Yudkovitz said.

One example of TiVo's advertising showcase was tied to the 2002 Mike Myers movie *Austin Powers in Goldmember*. When commercials for the film appeared during live TV, an icon offering the opportunity for more information appeared on the screens of TiVo subscribers. If they clicked on it, the show they were watching was paused and they were offered more options related to the film comedy. These included interviews with cast members, outtakes from the film, and the opportunity to enter a contest to have dinner with Myers. Those who enter such contests are considered qualified leads by advertisers because they have, in essence, asked to interact with the brand. TiVo is able to give advertisers detailed information on how many people watched the ad, for how long, which parts of the country they live in, and how old they are. It's a marriage of brand image advertising and direct marketing, bringing consumers closer to closing the loop with a purchase than a traditional commercial can.

"That is the kind of efficiency and targeting and accountability and measurement that advertisers have been screaming for," Yudkovitz said. "And you know what? It works."

About 6 months after Yudkovitz took over TiVo, I had breakfast with him in New York and asked him to explain his strategy and his philosophy on the evolution of the TV business. In his view, TV is about to enter its third age. The first was dominated by broadcast television. The second was the cable revolution, which vastly expanded consumer choice, upping the options from three channels to a dozen to 40 and now to several hundred for subscribers to digital cable or satellite TV. The third will be about consumer control and convenience.

"One of the consequences of so much choice is that TV became somewhat inconvenient, or at least a little bit unmanageable. And so new technology, placed in the hands not of the industry but of the consumer, started to change that. The electronic program guide made it much easier to start to get your arms around hundreds of channels, what's on," Yudkovitz said. "Video on demand obviously is going to make movies and other programming available on your own schedule, and DVR clearly was in the forefront of not only watching what you want when you want, but—and this is something people don't understand—finding what you want in the first place."

As revolutionary as DVR technology is, Yudkovitz conceded that change will come about relatively slowly, and that TiVo will have to learn to adapt if it hopes to survive.

"It unquestionably, fundamentally changes television, never to return to the old days, and it will roil the business model, but it will happen slowly, the same way second-generation happened," he said, noting that cable TV was around for well over a decade before the business took it seriously as a medium for choice and targeted programming, not just as a pathway to better broadcast reception.

According to Yudkovitz, some lessons were learned during cable's rise. "The people who fight it lose ground; the people who embrace it have a chance to gain ground. Cable didn't ruin anything, it changed the business model. There is plenty of money to be made, but models definitely change, economics definitely shift."

TiVo, Yudkovitz argued, can be used not just to skip ads but to enhance them—with targeting, long-form content, audience measurement, and interactive capabilities. His strategy is to enlist the support of marketers, ad agencies, and media specialists, and convince them that, if DVRs are inevitable, TiVo is the most ad-friendly solution. If they buy in, they can pressure broadcasters, cable operators, and satellite TV providers to work with TiVo.

"There's great resistance," Yudkovitz candidly admitted. "No matter what the technology is, you're dealing with the entrenched dynamics of an industry that don't move simply because someone built a better mousetrap. The economics of the business models make it such that change comes about slowly, begrudgingly."

Ad industry resistance to DVRs comes not only from true skeptics, but also from the "not on my watch" crowd, which wants to at least slow consumer adoption of the technology. Winning over cable systems such as Cablevision, Comcast, and Time Warner Cable is also a tremendous challenge. Although they have embraced DVRs, most of them have developed their own versions. Yudkovitz believes that they view TiVo's strong brand as a liability, fearing that the service could grow arrogant and make unreasonable financial demands, as ESPN did when it raised the fees it charged cable systems because viewers had to have the sports network.

As a result, he said, TiVo can't afford to be seen as a bully. "We have to cede control" to cable operators, Yudkovitz admitted.

But the real reasons for cable systems' resistance are more complex than that. Cable systems operators have a tendency to protect the exclusivity of their access to subscribers fiercely. And TiVo is available through satellite TV provider (and cable rival) DirecTV, which was acquired by Rupert Murdoch's News Corporation in 2003 and is expected to grow significantly in the coming years. TiVo has helped DirecTV keep subscribers longer, reducing customer turnover, or churn, by two-thirds, according to Yudkovitz: from 1.5 percent a month to 0.5 percent. It also raises subscription revenues by $10 to $20 per home per month. "It's not surprising, because if you have a DVR you're more likely to subscribe to HBO and other premium services because you can record movies and watch them when you want."

By late 2003 TiVo, had passed 1 million subscribers, half through satellite TV and half through stand-alone boxes. It still believes in stand-alone boxes, including new ones that combine DVR software with DVD players/recorders. And Yudkovitz at that point still believed that he could cut deals with cable systems, even though some industry observers see that as a long shot.

"It is not early," he conceded, "but, fortunately, it is not too late. The advertising guys are not talking to the cable guys about which DVR technology they want, saying, 'If you're going to adopt a DVR, you'd better adopt one that has our sensitivities in mind, which means one that not only skips commercials but enhances them.' I am trying to close this gap and create awareness that there is an upside."

TiVo employs a sales force to offer "enhanced" advertising to automakers and movie studios, but the company would rather turn that function over to TV networks and cable operators, saying that it sells the ads only because no one else wants to.

While there are some who question whether TiVo will be able to maintain its dominance as cable systems offer their own DVRs, Yudkovitz, not surprisingly, focuses on the fact that TiVo as the leader is still the one to beat.

"We're the hit show," he said, toward the end of our meeting in New York. "Everybody else is the knock-off, trying to be a hit."

Chapter 8

Movie Madness

Nothing has had as profound an impact on the business of making movies as the blood sport known as the opening weekend box office. The amount of money received from selling tickets during a film's first three days of wide release determines whether a picture is a hit or a flop. The stakes are big: Hollywood today is dominated by fewer than 10 studios, which include Walt Disney Co.'s Buena Vista, Sony, Warner Bros., Universal, 20th Century Fox, Miramax, Paramount, and New Line Cinema. They release about 500 films in the United States each year that take in some $9.5 billion at the box office. But even as ticket sales continue to rise, there is pressure on profit margins, which remain in the single digits for many studios.

It wasn't always this way, of course. In much of the second half of the twentieth century, movies made their debuts in New York and Los Angeles and played for weeks before being slowly rolled out to the rest of the country. There weren't that many theaters in the country, so it could be months before all the people who wanted to see a movie had had the chance to do so. Marketing was almost secondary, and marketing plans could take a long-term view, adjusting creative messages and media buys based on audiences' reactions to different plot points. If ads running during late-night talk shows didn't seem to be selling the film to young men as a comedy, the commercials could be changed to appeal to women by emphasizing the film's romantic elements, and the spots could be run during daytime soaps.

That was then. The rise of the multiplex and the proliferation of movie screens changed everything, making it possible for a movie to open across the country on the same date and for just about everybody who wanted to see the film the first night to find a seat. In 1980, there were 17,590 screens in the United States, according to the Motion Picture Association. By 2002, that number had soared to 35,280 screens at some 6000 theaters. The opening weekend began to account for a disproportionate percentage of a film's total domestic box-office take. *Spider-Man*, the top-grossing film of 2002, took in $115 million in its opening weekend, more than 25 percent of its total U.S. take of $403 million.

In addition, the consumer media caught on. No longer did the opening weekend grosses appear just in the pages of the trade magazine *Variety*. Now they were trumpeted on Sunday evening newscasts, which declared winners and losers, and in the pages of every newspaper and entertainment magazine. Even a disappointing performance could be made to seem solid if it was enough to earn the top ranking for a given weekend against weak competition. "Everybody has an opinion about what we do, and virtually none of them have a sense of really what they're talking about," said one studio executive.

The more important the opening weekend was, the more sophisticated the industry's marketing tools became. Marketing budgets skyrocketed along with production budgets as filmgoers demanded more and more bells and whistles. The average cost of producing a film rose from $9.4 million in 1980 to nearly $60 million in 2002. Marketing costs rose sharply as well, from $4 million in 1980 to more than $30 million, about half of which is spent on television ads. Profits became harder to achieve, with many films losing money in their U.S. runs (in 2002 the average box office per film was $32.5 million) and not seeing black ink until the movie was playing in scores of countries and had been released on DVD and videocassette. *Harry Potter and the Chamber of Secrets* sold $253 million worth of tickets in the United States, and another $476 million in the rest of the world.

"The film industry has really shifted over the last decade to become a totally focused marketing-driven operation," said Marc Shmuger, the vice chairman of Universal Studios and one of the most respected marketing executives in the film business. "As the opening weekend has become a greater and greater percentage of the overall revenue that a picture's going to take in, we've ended up front-loading our business."

There can be serious downsides to that, not just for the studios but also for the public, which can be misled by marketing noise and flock to theaters for a film that turns out to be awful. In most cases, the studios worry less than they used to about bad word of mouth, since their goal is getting seats filled during the first weekend; it's the rare hit that's able to build slowly on positive word of mouth, although when that happens, it can still be a powerful phenomenon. *My Big Fat Greek Wedding*, a 2002 independent comedy that went on to top $100 million in U.S. ticket sales, was a great example.

Also, studios have become less willing to take risks and have been shifting their focus to "franchise films," a fancy phrase for movies with sequel potential or those based on popular characters or story lines with built-in fan bases. Think *The Hulk*, *Charlie's Angels*, and *The Matrix*.

The franchises became known as tentpoles because they propped up studios' bottom lines. The profits from one strong tentpole can cover the losses of a half-dozen clunkers with change to spare. But the reliability of franchises and sequels was suddenly and surprisingly called into question in the summer of 2003, when many filmgoers seemed to reject such uninspired, recycled fare as *The Hulk* in favor of more original offerings such as the zombie thriller *28 Days Later*, which cost $8 million to make and sold $45 million in tickets.

Shmuger pointed out both the upsides and the downsides of the opening-weekend system. "There's more excitement attending that event than ever before, and I think that's something very appealing to marketers out there and something very beneficial to us," he said. On the other hand, he noted, the summer of 2003 showed "that the promise we were offering was far outstripping the reality of the experience we ended up giving audiences. That starts to take its toll on your audience over time, if you continue to do that."

The current realities make the movie business a rough enough terrain. Although studios spend often 10 to 20 times as much on marketing as music labels do, they need more and more marketing support from partners to increase their reach and contain their costs. There are even more frightening dangers looming on the horizon, namely the threat of digital piracy. It will never be as easy to download and trade a 2-hour motion picture over the Internet as it is to swap a 3-minute audio music file. But as more U.S. homes add high-speed Internet connections and advances are made in digital compression technologies, it will become far simpler, and no doubt there are millions of movie buffs who would be delighted to download films to their computers. The film industry, having learned the dangers of complacency by watching as the music business was upended by illegal file sharing, has been more aggressive in its response. Its tactics to combat piracy have included a paid advertising campaign featuring stuntmen, camera operators, and others who earn a blue-collar living from the movie business (since it would be difficult to muster sympathy for celebrities who pull in as much as $20 million per film) appealing to the public not to take food from their mouths by violating copyrights and stealing movies.

Also like the music business, the Hollywood studios have recognized that another way to help right their business plans is to enlist the deep-pocketed, marketing-savvy support of advertisers. The main question is, how much are they willing to give back in return?

Chapter 9

Producing an Answer

"The best car commercial ever," Joe Morgenstern wrote in *The Wall Street Journal*. His reference wasn't to a popular Volkswagen or Saturn ad, but to Paramount's remake of a 1960s cult classic, *The Italian Job*, a big-budget film that had just opened in theaters. Surprisingly, that line wasn't meant as a slap, but as something of a compliment. Morgenstern's review went on to call the action thriller "an absolute triumph of product placement, and great fun as a movie in the bargain."

The starring role held by the Mini, a tiny British sports car that had been imported to the United States, in *The Italian Job* was indeed a triumph of product placement, one that was viewed with awe and envy by players in Hollywood and on Madison Avenue.

The Italian Job tells the story of a group of thieves who set up a sting to get back at another baddie who double-crossed them after a daring heist. Key to their plan is a group of small, speedy cars that are capable of maneuvering in spaces where most other autos, especially the jumbo SUVs so popular in the United States, could never fit. The Minis were nothing less than characters in the film, as cool and sexy as lead actors Mark Wahlberg and Charlize Theron. It was a role that simply could not have been played by any other car, if for no other reason than physical specifications: The Minis in the movie performed stunts few cars could, turning tight circles in small indoor spaces, climbing nimbly down the stairs of a subway station, even riding the rails. And looking cool the whole time.

There was another reason that the filmmakers had little choice but to cast the Mini in the role: The original 1969 movie starring Michael Caine used British Minis, and devout fans of the cult classic would have rejected a replacement vehicle.

BMW, which produces the Mini, didn't pay a fee to participate in the film, but it did agree to custom-build 32 cars for the production. Tera Hanks, president of product-placement specialist Davie-Brown Entertainment, said the deal enabled the film to be made. "There's no way they could have [afforded to make] that movie. They couldn't have bought 32 cars without a true partnership with the folks from Mini. It was well over $1 million worth of vehicles."

The makers of *The Italian Job* had been hoping to time the launch of the film to the introduction of the car in the United States, but the script wasn't finished on time, so the studio never sought a formal tie-in with the automaker. Once the film was ready to go into production, however, it approached Mini about getting cars for the film.

It was no easy task. There were only 70 Mini dealers in the United States, and each dealer had only two of the cars. The filmmakers got permission from auto executives in Munich to stop production of U.S. Minis at a plant in Oxford in order to build 32 cars to the filmmakers' specifications. They also ordered crates of spare parts—windshield wipers, bumpers, tires, and the like—to repair cars damaged by stunt driving.

Davie-Brown arranged a series of promotional stunts to display the car's tie-in with the film. There was a segment on NBC's morning *Today* show about it, a Web site, and a big public-relations push. Mini enthusiasts were invited to drive their vehicles from all over the country to attend a screening of the film. But no promotional pact was ever inked, and, to the studio's chagrin, Mini did not buy any ads to promote the film or its involvement in it. "Paramount was really upset about it," said Ms. Hanks. "In the United States, the Mini wasn't an established brand, and they were afraid because they were still working on establishing the brand identity. In the international market, Mini is a cool, classic car that already has a strong identity."

The Mini deal itself was somewhat unique, but the presence of branded products in films has become commonplace. In some cases, the deals are still simple product placements—a marketer provides free products, which help studios lower the cost of dressing the sets, in exchange for an on-camera presence. But in most cases, these deals have become more strategic and complex. Marketers are getting involved much earlier in script development in order to control how their products are presented and create high-profile opportunities for exposure. And they are using their own marketing dollars and promotional muscle to drive moviegoers into theaters to see the films. When a live-action version of Dr. Seuss's *The Cat in the Hat* hit theaters for the 2003 holiday season, it was widely panned by critics as awful and nearly unwatchable. Yet, thanks largely to high-profile marketing tie-ins with more than half a dozen companies, including Burger King, Kraft, Kellogg's, Hershey, and five Procter & Gamble household brands (Cascade, Dawn, Febreze, Mr. Clean, and Swiffer), all of which ran ads featuring characters and gadgets from the film, the movie dominated the box office in its opening weekend.

"The entertainment content company and the consumer product brand company have each come to recognize they do need each other, or they need help, and they suspect that the other may be able to help them," said Universal Studios Vice Chairman Marc Shmuger.

The number of ambitious marketer-movie alliances has soared in recent years. General Motors' Pontiac tied in with the Revolution Studios spy movie *XXX*, starring Vin Diesel, in the summer of 2002. The lead character in the film drove a 1967 GTO, and Pontiac wanted to promote the 2004 relaunch of the car by building awareness among young people. For the theatrical release, and again for the release of the film on DVD, it ran sweepstakes backed by advertising support. The tie-in helped the movie make $145 million at the U.S. box office.

In some cases, the deals are with studios rather than being for individual films. Miramax and Coors formed a partnership that gives Coors an early look at scripts and the first opportunity to be a tie-in partner. For example, the Coors twins, sexy female characters who appear in Coors ads, made an appearance in the Miramax film *Scary Movie 3*. (That tie-in wound up being criticized because the film earned a PG-13 rating, meaning that kids under the drinking age were allowed in to see a movie that featured characters best known for promoting beer.) Revolution Studios formed a similar nonexclusive alliance with Ford Motor Company that gives the automaker an early look at films before they begin shooting.

As studios and marketers become more comfortable with each other, the alliances are becoming more complex. Increasingly, advertisers are asking to film commercials for their tie-ins while the movie is being filmed, shooting original footage that uses the same locations, sets, actors, and costumes. Those who think this is a good idea agree that it is fairly simple to send out a "second unit" film crew to shoot such footage during breaks in the regular shooting schedule. That's exactly what happened with a tie-in between Jeep and the Paramount film *Tomb Raider II: Cradle of Life.*

Jeep created three special vehicles for use in the film (and later use in Jeep promotions as part of a tour). In exchange, Jeep was able to shoot commercials touting its tie-in on location, using the same sets as the filmmakers. After months of negotiations, it even got the film's star, Angelina Jolie, to appear in ads. The key to the deal was an agreement that she would appear in the ads in her Lara Croft character, making the fictional film heroine the spokeswoman for Jeep and (in theory) protecting the actress's image. She also refused to end the commercial by saying, "It's a Jeep thing," the tag line the ad team originally wanted. Instead, she says, "Let's see them catch me now," before speeding away from the bad guys in her tricked-out Jeep Wrangler Rubicon.

Some people believe that the tie-ins need to go even deeper, that, as with TV shows, the answer is for marketers to actually take ownership positions in films, to participate in both the risks and the profits. Among other hurdles, this will require marketers to commit to films as much as 3 years before they hit theaters. That would necessitate a new discipline for brand marketers, who are often reluctant to make plans more than a year in advance. Universal's Marc Shmuger, though, is among those who believe that deeper partnerships are necessary. Studios need to "work with brands so we're not force-feeding them our already-baked product," he said during a speech at an entertainment marketing conference in Los Angeles, asking, "Can we co-create?" He suggested that brand marketers allot a portion of their research and development budgets to script development.

The entertainment industry's future hinges on the collective brainpower of those in charge. Many of them are savvy and creative, and all of them are aware of the challenges their town faces. Watching them figure it out over the next few years is sure to be Hollywood's most engaging and entertaining production.

Chapter 10

BMW's Powder Keg

The film opens with grainy footage from a hand-held camera. In an unidentified Central American country, soldiers with automatic weapons line up villagers—men, women, and children—in a field and systematically massacre them. From the tall grass can be heard the soft clicks of a camera belonging, we are to learn, to an American photojournalist named Harvey Jacobs, who has secretly captured images of the grisly shootings.

The viewers aren't the only ones who pick up on the camera's whirrs. In seconds, soldiers who have overheard the sound are shouting and running into the grass, firing their rifles as they pursue the photographer. Despite being wounded by gunfire, he manages to escape to a nearby village and find temporary refuge in the home of sympathizers. Tensions run high. "Get that damn gringo out of here or we're going to be screwed," a woman hisses in Spanish to a man in the safe house.

The photographer is soon picked up by a man from the American Embassy, who hustles him into the back seat of a sport utility vehicle and heads for the border, transporting him (and his film) toward safety and medical attention. As they drive, they pass scenes of human suffering and misery—children begging for food, prostitutes working the corners, soldiers patting down young men against the sides of buildings. "What are we doing to this country?" Jacobs asks the driver. "All this so yuppies can have their weekly line of coke."

But the driver is distracted, glancing into his rearview mirror at a pickup truck that is clearly in pursuit of his vehicle. The chase is on, and the SUV is soon flying at 80 miles per hour along narrow, twisting mountain roads crowded with military trucks and slow-moving farm equipment. When his credentials are questioned at a checkpoint, the driver suddenly throws his vehicle into reverse, violently smashing the front end of the pursuing truck, and speeds off the road as bullets shatter a side window and crash into cargo door.

When he pulls back onto the road moments later, all is peaceful—they are safely across the border. "We made it, Harvey, we made it," he shouts excitedly. But the photographer has slumped across the back seat, which is slick with his blood. He is lifeless. "Shit," the driver screams, smashing his fist repeatedly against the rear seat, soaking himself in blood. "Shit."

Cut to the exterior of a middle-class American home. The driver has sought out the mother of his passenger. He awkwardly informs her that her son has been posthumously awarded a Pulitzer Prize, then delivers the dog tags the journalist had been wearing around his neck when he was shot. He presses the medallion into the mother's hands, and the elderly, blind woman runs her fingers along the Braille type there. She begins to cry as she reads this last message from her son, and she backs slowly into her home, closing the door. The driver turns and walks off into a blinding sun.

This movie, *Powder Keg*, was beautifully shot— on location in the United States and Mexico—and featured high production values, a haunting soundtrack, and solid acting performances. It was directed by the acclaimed filmmaker Alejandro Gonzalez-Inarritu. The driver was played by the handsome British actor Clive Owens. But the film didn't win any Academy Awards—not for its screenplay, its direction, its acting, its music, or its cinematography.

In fact, it wasn't even nominated.

In fact, it wasn't even a movie.

It was an ad, a 10-minute commercial designed to show off the speed, handling, braking power, and off-road capabilities of BMW's X5 sport utility vehicle.

It was, perhaps, the future of advertising.

In the nascent Madison & Vine space, few initiatives have captured people's imaginations the way the BMW Films series has. It quickly became the model for advertising as entertainment, a prototype for a new form of advertising, and a case study in what can happen when one company has the nerve to challenge conventional wisdom, ignore the rules, and create a new business model.

It also stirred debate. Critics questioned whether the ads were effective, whether they could be called good advertising, whether they, in fact, could even be called ads.

BMW of North America financed eight mini-films over a 2-year period in 2001 and 2002. The films were the brainchild of its ad agency, a brash Minneapolis-based shop known as Fallon, after its founder, Pat Fallon, and well respected for its creativity. They were brought to life through the work of, among others, a commercial production operation called Anonymous Content.

Each film in "The Hire" series was under the control of a top Hollywood director, and there typically was tremendous star power in front of the cameras as well. There was Tony Scott's *Beat the Devil*, starring James Brown as a singer who has sold his soul to the devil (played in a deliciously over-the-top performance by Gary Oldman) and wins it back in a drag race in the Las Vegas desert. There was Guy Ritchie's comical *Star*, which featured the director's real-life wife, actress/singer Madonna, as a Hollywood A-lister with a monstrous ego who is humbled and humiliated during a nightmare ride to a movie premiere that ends with her being unceremoniously dumped on the red carpet, a disheveled mess, in front of a phalanx of paparazzi. John Woo, Ang Lee, and John Frankenheimer also directed films in the series. Clive Owens starred as "The Driver" in each.

To attract such blue-chip talent, BMW knew that it had to break its own rules and guarantee the directors near-total creative control. That's a difficult idea for any advertiser to swallow. Usually the client is boss. If the client wants the logo in ads made bigger, or the camera to linger lovingly on the product for a few more seconds, it has the power to make that happen. The ad agency creatives shooting the commercials may grumble, and even threaten to walk, but they ultimately work in a client service business. Advertisers control the message, from when it leaves their hands until it hits consumers' eyeballs.

This was different. Securing the best directors in Hollywood meant letting them do things that might make the BMW executives squirm. Like having a character bleed to death in the back seat of one of the vehicles.

Jim McDowell, vice president of marketing at BMW of North America, said that he and his team never dreamed of tinkering with the creative process. "From our early work with the James Bond films, there is no way that we were ever going to change a script," McDowell said. His reference was to BMW's late 1990s tie-ins with a trio of James Bond films.

> There were some things about scripts that made us quite uncomfortable, and through discussions back and forth we learned to deal with discomfort. Particularly the second James Bond film, which had a 7-series in the script that flew off of the side of the parking garage and ended up in an Avis rental car showroom. We seriously had a debate about [this;] we didn't want to see our car falling seven stories and [being]

destroyed. We began to learn that there were things that were more important about telling a good story than necessarily having it exactly the way that the car company wanted.

With the film series, McDowell said,

We knew, if were going to get the likes of a Frankenheimer or an Ang Lee to do it, we would have to give them a tremendous amount of artistic license. In every instance, the directors came forward with such wonderful insights of what the film could be to make it really compelling entertainment. Did they do things that we would have not done the same way if it had been ourselves? Yes. Would the work have been better if it had been changed the way we would have done it? No. Because we understood that boundary.

There was yet another catch. The films didn't appear in theaters, although theatrical trailers for the films did, trailers that were designed to look just like the "Coming Attractions" for feature-length movies. They didn't appear on TV, either, at least not at first. Instead, BMW put the films on the Internet and invited viewers to come to its site to download them.

In advertising, this amounted to heresy. Viewers don't seek out ads. Ads seek out viewers; they intrude on the viewers' eyeballs and brains as they consume media. And people don't like ads. To ask consumers to voluntarily seek out an advertising message, then devote time and space on their computer hard drive to downloading the ads before spending even more time watching them, was risky. BMW was also running over another sacred cow: In order to get the production values it wanted for the videos, it had to reverse its budget ratios. Typically an advertiser will spend 10 percent of its ad budget to produce its commercials and 90 percent to "distribute" them to consumers—to buy advertising time and space on TV networks, magazines, newspapers, billboards, and the like. But to produce high-quality films that were up to its technical and aesthetic standards, BMW had to commit to spending a shocking 90 percent of its ad budget on production. That left just 10 percent to promote the films, to lure prospective customers to its Web site to download and view them. It did that with some TV and newspaper ads, but also with commercials in movie theaters that mimicked film trailers. BMW won't discuss what it spent on the films, but based on past spending patterns and conversations with executives involved in the films, $15 million seems like a solid estimate. Based on that figure, BMW spent just $1.5 million to promote the films, and a whopping $13.5 million to produce them.

It seemed like it could never work. Except that it did.

To understand the success of the films, it's important to understand the context in which they were created. In a case study that appeared in *Advertising Age*'s *Madison & Vine* newsletter in 2002, reporters Kate MacArthur and Jean Halliday wrote,

It was 2000, and the luxury automaker had become trapped in its Gordon Gekko/'80s image and its performance-oriented advertising touting the "Ultimate Driving Machine" was copied to the point of category monotony. Moreover, BMW's affluent and busy consumer base was watching far less network TV than its media buys reflected. When Fallon presented brand campaign concepts for 2001, both sides agreed that since there was no specific product launch, it was time for BMW to take the gloves off and let the agency have more freedom. Spurred by the insight that 85% of BMW's customers were using the Internet to research car buys, Fallon asked BMW to take a chance on a new idea.

David Lubars, president and executive creative director of Fallon, takes it from there: "We knew this would either be hugely successful or a complete failure." What Fallon was asking its client to do was stunning in terms of inverting the traditional advertising model.

The BMW Films became an Internet phenomenon. Internet-savvy people, many a lot younger and far more impressionable than the carmaker's typical buyers, passed the word to friends by email and in chat rooms. BMW had to add more servers to meet the demand for the downloads. Working in its favor, the automaker's upscale audience was more likely to have high-speed Internet connections at work and at home, so the download times were not nearly as painful as they were for those who tried to pull in the film files over slower dial-up connections.

Film viewings soared into the millions, then into the tens of millions. And the ads seemed to work. Consumer research showed that BMW's image in the marketplace was being strengthened, particularly among younger shoppers, and that the car was showing up on more car-buying wish lists. Visits to dealerships soared, and—most important—so did U.S. sales. BMW sold a record 213,127 vehicles in the United States in 2001, up 12.5 percent over the previous year, and it beat its own records again in 2002 and 2003, despite a sharp downturn in the U.S. economy and the relatively high price of its performance cars.

In June of 2003, the BMW Films were inducted into the permanent collection of the Museum of Modern Art. So they were art. But were they advertising?

The question feels stale, having been endlessly chewed over for 2 years by pundits and awards-show juries. Yet the debate persists, reflecting the reluctance of some in the industry to accept branded content as a legitimate marketing tool. After all, it's much less disruptive to treat such initiatives as one-shots, passing fads, or experiments. Even those who liked the films claimed that they could work only for advertisers with narrow target audiences, such as BMW, and that most advertisers wouldn't have the nerve to risk their marketing budgets on such things or that they'd lose if they did take the gamble.

The industry couldn't decide, or was afraid to, how to treat BMW Films. The world's most prestigious advertising awards show, held each year in Cannes, France, and attended by thousands of advertising creatives and executives from around the globe, barred BMW Films from its film competition the first year, barely escaping with its credibility when it awarded the series a shared top prize in the Internet category.

After an outcry, the International Advertising Festival created a new awards category the following year to, as jury president Dan Wieden noted, recognize work that "causes the industry to reconsider the way forward." But the award felt false, seeming to have been blatantly designed to recognize BMW's creative achievement and its contribution to the development of a new advertising form, while at the same time perpetuating the ghettoization of branded entertainment.

"It's a nice gesture," I wrote in a column in *Advertising Age* at the time, "but it will encourage those who want to continue to treat breakthrough creative concepts as creatures separate from the almighty 30-second spot."

Clearly, the BMW Films were a next step in the development of advertising through entertainment.

"We're not talking about product placement, we're not talking about brand-sponsored programming, what we're talking about is brand integration," said Mitch Kanner, who oversees the entertainment marketing practice at the Hollywood talent agency The Firm. "If we look at BMW Films, developed to be a brand integration piece, most of them were spot-on perfect. You never saw a beauty shot of a car, you never heard anybody talk about the vehicle. But what they did was they exhibited all of the personality features so perfectly. You see a film like *Powder Keg*, where it's about a devastating massacre of 100 people, you never see a beauty shot of the car. The victim bleeds all over the car, there's profanity.

"But at the end of the day, when you realize that you just watched a BMW film, you say, 'Holy shit, the car delivered.' That 'holy shit' is the factor that we have to try to create nowadays."

Chapter 11

Under the Hood

As with many success stories, there is no shortage of industry people—agency creatives, producers, consultants—who are eager and willing to take credit for the BMW Films concept. This baby, as they say, had a lot of parents.

But no one is more responsible for the films than the man who controlled the purse strings for BMW's advertising, and who put his own career and credibility on the line when he approved what seemed to be a hare-brained scheme to promote his product. That man is Jim McDowell, a soft-spoken gentleman who runs U.S. marketing for BMW but who on first glance—he is always sharply dressed and wears stylish glasses—looks more like a college professor than a peddler of sports cars.

McDowell was always respected in the automotive business for his marketing prowess, but the BMW Films series brought him a new level of business-world fame, not to mention an office full of awards and momentos, such as the framed gold jacket worn by James Brown in *Beat the Devil.*

I visited with McDowell in his glass-walled office at BMW's U.S. headquarters in a leafy New Jersey suburb to view the BMW Films initiative through his eyes and to question him about why it worked and what it meant for advertising's future.

McDowell led up to BMW Films by first providing context on BMW as a marketer and on its target audience.

> What we have always believed in terms of our marketing is that we want to go out and have a serious interaction with relatively a handful of people to be able to sell 240,000 cars. We have a relatively high amount of loyalty to start with, so that means in a given year maybe we need to go out and find 100,000 new purchasers. Some companies would try and have a very casual involvement with millions of people to get the 100,000 new purchasers. We are a little more specific. We're trying to say, since we know so much about the psychographic of who we appeal to, we should be able to get quite close to a much smaller group of people and then have a much bigger form of involvement with them.

So BMW has never been a typical marketer. Unlike, say, a maker of mayonnaise, which needs to get its commercial message in front of as many people as possible, BMW can set its sights on a narrower target and go at those prospective buyers hard. And it does that, offering the people it targets such goodies as a free professional driving course with a $300 value, confident of the return it will get on that hefty investment, confident of the likelihood that it can convert that person racing around the track to a buyer of its vehicles.

As McDowell talks, he frequently jumps enthusiastically from his chair to seek out a prop to illustrate the point he is making. Describing a demonstration of the BMW X5's hill-climbing capabilities, he held toy ramps against the side of a toy tractor-trailer and told how the vehicle went up and over the truck at sharp angles. "We have a history of trying to create really fun things that people can do with the BMW," he said. "We have tried to have communications that were distinctive from the rest of the marketplace."

In that context, it's perhaps not so surprising that Fallon would take a chance on presenting its client with such a radical idea. And BMW had been involved with the entertainment business before. For the 1996 introduction of its Z3 roadster, it inked a pact for the sports car to be anointed the new vehicle of the fictional secret agent James Bond. "We knew this car was absolutely going to be a hit, so [we] decided we could spend our money to launch it a traditional way, but that this was probably one car that could get away with very little in the way of launch expenditure. We could do a regular launch, or aim for a higher goal."

He chose the latter path. The role of James Bond was being taken over by Pierce Brosnan with 1996's *GoldenEye*, and MGM, the studio that releases the Bond films, was giving Bond a makeover to update an image that seemed stale and old-fashioned. Among other things, the spy was trading in his Aston Martin for a BMW.

The car had only a small role in the film, but BMW played its involvement to the hilt. It shot a commercial in which a British lord, addressing his peers, warns them of "a development that shakes the bedrock of what is Britain," which turned out to be the news of Bond's new car.

Although it paid to produce and air the commercials, BMW didn't pay a penny to participate in the film. Instead, its commercials served to promote the movie and extend its marketing budget indirectly. Even the production costs of the commercials were held down, since BMW was given access to finished scenes from the film for use in the ads without having to shoot new footage or pay the actors endorsement fees (a loophole that, McDowell admits, didn't endear the carmaker to Brosnan, whose only compensation was a free high-end BMW).

After the Bond tie-ins—BMW cars and motorcycles also made appearances in 1997's *Tomorrow Never Dies* and 1999's *The World Is Not Enough*—the automaker went looking for the next big thing, the idea that would allow it to differentiate itself from the competitive pack. McDowell decided to issue a challenge to his agency: Create a marketing campaign to demonstrate that "what your car does well, a BMW does brilliantly." If he expected to be dazzled by his agency, and he did, McDowell knew he would have to free it from the restraints that all advertisers place on their marketing partners. He would have to give Fallon permission to let its imagination run wild.

Late in 2000, the BMW marketing team drafted a letter to its ad agency that amounted to a "What if?" challenge: What if the automaker were to remove some of the restrictions, allow its agency to lose the rulebook, and toss out shackles such as retaining a consistent look and feel for all BMW communications. McDowell told his shop, "We will allow you to selectively violate some of those rules on this one project if it will enable you to come forward with something much more interesting that will have a greater impact."

Fallon responded to the challenge. It came back to BMW with the idea for a series of short films (it was thinking 30 minutes at the time; this was eventually reduced to 10) directed by leading Hollywood directors and distributed digitally over the Internet.

As far out as the deal may have seemed to some, McDowell says he embraced it fairly quickly, recognizing that if they were done right, the films would appeal to BMW's target audience.

> We weren't terribly worried that we would make this thing work. We just didn't know if we would have to go to Plan B or Plan C because we were confident that working with Fallon and our partners in the industry, we would come up with five good films, and we were relatively confident,

based on what we had done leveraging the James Bond promotions, that we could get word out there in an interesting way that we had these films, and enough people would come and see them. But we pretty much had a break-even point in mind, that we had to get at least 2 million film views or the economics of what we were doing didn't make sense. The question was, what happens if you only get 1 million film views? Because then you've spent all the money on the creative but it [has] cost us twice as much as you anticipated for people to see one of your films.

Still, BMW did come up with other plans for distributing the films in case Internet downloads peaked at 1 million, plans such as showing the films on airplanes or distributing them on DVDs. Although it eventually followed through with several of those alternative delivery plans—the films ran as programming on cable TV's Bravo network and were available through the Bloomberg financial-information terminals that sit on the desks of Wall Street traders—this was icing on the cake at that point. The films by then had far surpassed any original goals.

Although McDowell said that he quickly sold the idea to upper management at BMW, he admits that a lot of people in the company were kept in the dark, in part to avoid rivals knowing of the plan beforehand and ripping it off, and in part to avoid a messy public debate over how advertising dollars should be allocated.

"We knew this was bold, absolutely unbelievable. We knew that unless you sat down and explained it properly, almost everyone would say this was totally absurd," McDowell said. "But we have a company culture that really encourages BMW to be the first to do something, not a quick follower. We believe we just need to appeal to this particular psychographic, and it truly doesn't matter what the rest of the world thinks as long as our prospects think it's cool."

The first film, John Frankenheimer's *Ambush*, was released in April 2001. BMW's marketing strategy was referred to internally as "whisper to shout." The company felt that the most important first audience for the films was Hollywood's creative community. If the writers, directors, and producers of top feature films gave a thumbs-up to the movies—not as car ads, but as short films, as art even—it would give them a new level of respectability.

BMW released a new film every 3 weeks. Initially, it relied heavily on word of mouth to build buzz. But with each new release it raised the level of marketing support, adding posters, for example, and later TV commercials and movie-theater ads. In newspapers, BMW ran ads in the entertainment section that looked a lot like ads for new theatrical film releases. The goal was to build interest in films that weren't showing in any theater, but were available to anyone with a computer and an Internet hookup.

By summer, the buzz around the films had built to a roar, with countless articles in newspapers and magazines such as *Time*, and stories on the evening news. (Not to mention communications over the

Internet, which brings new meaning to the concept of word of mouth, spreading news rapidly to millions of people.) Although BMW spent less than $2 million to promote the films, its public relations agency estimated that the news pickups added another $20 million in media value.

Remember that BMW's goal was to get 2 million downloads of the first film series. It ended up with 13 million.

It didn't stop there. After debating whether to bring the series back, BMW committed to a second season for 2002. When the new films were released, they were an instant hit. Downloads rapidly climbed from 13 million to 50 million.

I asked McDowell how BMW measured success beyond the number of downloads, pointing out that some critics of the programs complained that the automaker couldn't draw a direct connection between the film views and its sales success. Others argued that it may have changed the image of the car, but mostly among teens and college students, who might not yet have licenses to drive and certainly couldn't afford a BMW if they did.

Here again, McDowell proved that BMW travels a different path from many advertisers, that it certainly cares about proving the return on its marketing investment, but it also takes a long-term view of brand building that is somewhat out of vogue these days, when most publicly held companies face constant pressure to deliver quarterly sales growth.

I truly believe with a product as strong as ours, the role of marketing is to get people to put us on their shopping list for a product that they will purchase in the next cycle. Or even more broadly than that, the way that I prefer to say it is, my job is to send people to bed at night dreaming about a BMW. Maybe they will realize that dream in a couple of years. Maybe it'll be five years. But that's our job, really: to set this dream in place.

McDowell also believes that advertising ideas such as the short films can be more effective than TV precisely because consumers choose to seek out and view these films rather than having an ad intrude on them while they are watching a sitcom or the evening news.

A lot of people that you're paying for to watch your advertising on television may be actually vacuuming or ironing or in the kitchen getting something to eat at the time that your ad is on. I would argue that people are far more attentive watching something that they've worked hard to download on their computer than something that just happens to be in the same room that they are. So I look at it as there being a qualitative difference in terms of the level of interaction.

That's not to say that BMW didn't gauge the program's success using standard industry benchmarks. The carmaker keeps a close eye, as do its rivals, on "intent to purchase" research showing whether consumers intend to buy a new auto in the next 3 years and, if so, which auto brands are on their shopping lists. In the months after the release of the films, McDowell said, there was a noticeable uptick in BMW's numbers. There was also an uptick in the numbers that matter most: sales. BMW set U.S. sales records despite a recession and the September 11 terrorist attacks, which caused larger rivals such as General Motors to offer attractive concessions like zero percent financing to potential buyers.

Since a large number of people were skeptical about the success of BMW Films, I asked McDowell how he saw the naysayers—why, in his view, there was such resistance to what amounts to a creative idea in an industry that defines itself by its ability to develop breakthrough concepts.

"Big market share participants in the status quo are very reluctant to embrace the wave of the next great thing," McDowell said.

> They have become very good at maximizing their market share in an existing framework and existing marketplace, and when something new comes up that could actually put that into a setback, there is a certain amount of denial at the beginning.
>
> It's very interesting that Western Union didn't see much opportunity in telephones. Whoever is particularly good at a prior technology tends

to be slow at embracing the next new technology that might replace it. I think that was part of the issue. I think there was a certain skepticism about how real were the numbers, how qualified were the people that were coming to see the films.

BMW claims that viewers of the films had a median age of 31 and a median household income of $90,000, a respectable demographic that matched that of the prospective buyers of BMW's lower-end 3-series line of vehicles. There were a lot of high school– and college-age viewers, McDowell admits, but he says they were almost perfectly balanced on the other side by older, more affluent viewers—or, as he identified them, "5-series and 7-series prospects," potential buyers of higher-priced BMWs. "It was a fairly even distribution, and very wide."

On the one hand, McDowell realizes—relishes the thought, actually—that many advertisers couldn't easily follow in BMW's footsteps. But when it comes to the idea that the consumer is in control, and that marketers must find a way to get invited in by the consumer, he believes that any company that hopes to be doing business in the years ahead has little choice but to adapt.

As for BMW, while it may create another series of films, it's already on the prowl for the next big idea.

Over the years we have been really good at inviting people to do things, and we believe strongly that it is far more important to have a meaningful interaction with a handful of people than a casual interaction with a much larger group of people.

Chapter 12

Stop the Music

Here's what sets the music business apart from other segments of the entertainment industry: It has already been run over by a truck, and now it's struggling to get back on its feet. Whether it makes it or not will depend largely on whether it has the ability, and the guts, to undergo a painful reinvention of its business model.

The threats to the film and television industries, while real, are still somewhat theoretical, or at least not imminent. True, both of those industries' business models are showing cracks—TV audiences are fragmented, and film profits are threatened by skyrocketing production and marketing costs—but the real threats to their future viability are still somewhat off in the future. TV's real danger point will come when personal video recorders reach critical mass. The movie business lives in fear of technological advances that will allow millions of computer users to download films at no charge and watch them at home before they've even been released in theaters.

The music business is facing a different situation. Its problems are not a year off, not even a few months off. This is an industry that is already under attack, one that has been slammed by technology, one that is in perhaps the deepest slump in its history.

The cause of its pain: the Internet, which gave music consumers the ability to easily download and share music without paying for it and gave them the ability to reject the idea of albums (prepackaged bundles of about a dozen songs selling for upwards of $20) in favor of picking out only the songs they liked—again, without paying for them.

Music executives are among the most depressed and bewildered of entertainment industry types these days. Few of them bother to pretend that things are good. Even fewer pretend that they have a clue as to how to solve the industry's woes, although the business is getting more aggressive in answering challenges and confronting the impact that file sharing and piracy have had on sales of recorded music.

"Do you have any idea," a marketing executive at a major music label asked me one day by way of greeting, "how fucked it is to be in the record business these days?"

Actually, yes.

The troubles began midway through 1999, when a college dropout named Shawn Fanning introduced Napster, file-sharing software that enabled so-called peer-to-peer trading of digital music files online.

Essentially, users could download songs at no cost and trade them with others.

The service soon exploded, particularly on college campuses, where students often had free time and access to high-speed Internet connections. At its peak, Napster recorded more than 1.5 million visitors a day and logged 2.7 billion downloads each month, according to figures from Jupiter Research.

Although some supporters of illicit online file-trading services deny that they played a role in the industry's decline, there's no question that as music piracy rose, sales of recorded music sank. According to the Recording Industry Association of America, U.S. CD shipments fell 6.4 percent in 2001 and another 8.9 percent in 2002. A 2003 study by Edison Media Research found that people who reported downloading more than 100 songs also reported a steep drop in CD purchases.

The industry fought back, filing lawsuits against Napster for copyright infringement that were eventually successful. In February 2001, a federal court ended Napster's days as an illegal service when it ordered the company to stop trading copyrighted material. But that wasn't the end of peer-to-peer services. Other popular services soon took over from Napster, services with names such as Kazaa and Morpheus, and online users continued to download several billion songs each month without paying for them.

In addition to the suits against Napster, marketers of recorded music began to find other ways to combat piracy, which they blamed for decimating recorded music sales. There are factors in the decline beyond file-sharing sites and CD burners, of course. Even consumers who download songs legally reject buying an album when what they want is a single. Others say that product quality is more to blame—there's simply not enough good music. The industry disputes that.

"It's not a product problem," says Jimmy Iovine, who runs the Interscope/Geffen/A&M record labels for Universal Music Group and is one of the most respected and powerful talents in the music business. "Why would you have people downloading four billion songs a month it if was product? Let me tell you something: People don't even take stuff for free that they hate. You can give out bad hamburgers across the street, and nobody's going in there. They'd rather pay $1.50 for a good one. Is there a Renaissance moment going on right now in music, are we witnessing the birth of punk? No. But there is fabulous hip-hop and there are great records out there."

In Iovine's view, as in the view of many in the music business, there is a direct connection between online file sharing and the industry's woes. "You can't compete with convenience and free," he says. "If Diet Coke and Coke were coming out of people's kitchen faucets, their sales would go down. People wouldn't say, 'Let me go get in line at Costco to get my case of Coke' if they could say, 'Let me just turn the faucet on.' It's a gigantic problem."

Ultimately, it boils down to a marketing issue. It's almost impossible for artists to break through today. They can't get radio exposure. Stations are no longer really part of local communities and reflective of local tastes; instead, they belong to large consolidated radio groups that stick to a small, carefully market-researched playlist, cycling through a handful of bland pop tunes repeatedly. MTV, which used to be a major marketing tool because it aired videos that whetted teens' appetites for albums, has been transformed into a lifestyle network that airs reality shows filmed in beach houses and edgy cartoons about teen angst. Videos have been pushed to second-tier channels.

"The record companies, even before this down-turn in the last few years, never had the kind of marketing dollars that the marketplace demands now," says Rob Light, partner and head of the music practice at the Hollywood talent agency Creative Artists Agency. "They were kind of spoiled for the first 30 years of rock and roll, where radio was their marketer. And it was free."

> Now you have to find other ways to do it. And their marketing budgets didn't keep up with other brands. The Rolling Stones are a brand, just like McDonald's or eBay. But none of the music acts had the kind of ad campaigns behind them that those companies did.

There's a broad spectrum of possible solutions, but four primary paths are being explored by the music business. The first is to create high-quality, legitimate download services. Record executives believe that people will pay for music if they have choice and convenience. At first this didn't seem like an easy path. The record labels set up or supported sites such as

BuyMusic.com and Musicmatch. Even Napster was reinvented as a paid site. The idea was that subscribers would pay to download songs instead of essentially stealing them. However, in their earliest days, most of the legitimate sites weren't serious competitors to the likes of Kazaa. They often had smaller libraries of songs or put sharp restrictions on how songs could be copied, stored, and played.

Then, in April 2003, Apple Computer, a company known for innovation, introduced a paid subscription service called iTunes that immediately gave the music industry hope. Here, finally, was a serious challenger of the illegal sites. iTunes had a fully stocked catalogue of music, great design, and a simple navigation method. It sold singles for 99 cents, albums for $9.99. Songs could be played off computer hard drives or down-loaded into iPods, Apple's sleekly designed digital music player.

iTunes was an instant hit. Although it was initially available only to the less than 10 percent of computer users who have Apple machines, the service sold 1 million songs in just its first week. Within months, that figure hit 10 million. And that was before the intro-duction of a Windows version of iTunes that could be used by the vast majority of computer users. It took just 3 days for Windows users to hit 1 million iTunes downloads.

Once again, it's all about consumer empower-ment. Who wants to carry stacks of CDs in the car or a briefcase, or to have to sort through dozens of discs to find the one they want and then play it, when they can simply dial up any one of the thousands of songs they've got digitally filed on an iPod, which is smaller than a pack of cigarettes and has sound that rivals that of expensive home entertainment systems? The end user gets what she wants when she wants it, and she can carry her entire music collection around in her jacket pocket.

Of course, even here there are tremendous implications for how music is marketed and sold. The industry is heading back to the model of being more about singles than about albums, and that brings with it the threat of lower revenue and a revamped business model. But many executives believe that this is inevitable, another challenge that the industry simply must confront.

"Nobody stops and asks, 'How does an 8- or 9-year-old consumer consume music? What's the next generation going to buy?'" says CAA's Light. "By the time an 8-year-old is ready to buy music, he's never going to want a jewel box [the plastic cases in which CDs are stored]. He probably doesn't even listen to radio. He's probably streaming music" over the Internet. "The whole industry, because we're constantly moving, doesn't have the time to step back and go, 'How do we fix this?' We haven't given the consumer an alternative."

Light points out that by releasing singles on the radio 8 to 12 weeks before an album is in stores, the music industry is guilty of creating the demand for singles that it now wants to fight against. This is yet another example of how entertainment marketers, often for reasons that no one can easily explain, go to market in a different way from other marketers of consumer products.

You're promoting a single for 12 weeks. If you want it, you don't want to wait. You're telling me this is the song to like. I like it. I want it. It's a self-fulfilling prophecy that they're creating. Would you ever go sell the new McDonald's burger and not have it in the store? Isn't that what the record companies are doing for 12 weeks? It's a really strange dynamic because we are a society that loves instant gratification. We're going to have to rethink how we talk to the consumer.

After legitimate online services, the second possible solution to piracy is lawsuits against those who swipe music digitally, a strategy that risks alienating customers, but one that the industry finally pursued in the fall of 2003, when the Recording Industry Association of America filed suits against several hundred people, accusing them of downloading thousands of songs without paying for them. Although there was much initial hand-wringing over the move—the press salivated when it learned that a 12-year-old girl was among those being sued—within a month more than a hundred of those who had been targeted settled the suits by agreeing to apologize and paying fines of a few thousand dollars.

Miles Copeland, who runs the Ark 21 specialty music label and used to manage the pop singer Sting, supports the use of lawsuits despite the risk of alienating customers. "I can't compete with free, and I don't think any label can," Copeland says, citing the layoffs that have hit the music industry in recent years. "The record business has been so worried about offending the public. What's more offensive than having to fire half your staff? I think we've woken [people] up [to] the fact that theft is theft. So what if it's a 12-year-old? If she was a 12-year-old shoplifter, would you decide to let her walk out with a t-shirt?"

Although a few hundred lawsuits may deter some people, it would take a long time for the industry to catch up with the millions who use illegal sites. Still, says the music executive Iovine, the lawsuits are an important tool to educate parents of young computer users about the consequences of their actions.

"Property is property, whether material property or intellectual property, and if it's yours, you get to say what you're going to do with it," Iovine says. "Right now, the family is ignoring it. They're saying, 'Oh, everybody is doing it, and at least now [the kids] don't ask me to drive them to the record store and pay parking.' But sooner or later, the parents are going to say, 'All right, enough of this. Let's deal with someone legitimate. Let's find a way'" to legally download music.

The third path is price cuts. Universal Music Group, the largest record label, was the first to open that door, announcing in the fall of 2003 that it would lower the cost of its CDs by 30 percent to spur sales.

The fourth path is to align with brands to extend distribution and marketing budgets—the Madison & Vine expedition.

Chapter 13

Change That Tune

"Are you ready to go to the next level?"

That's the question a hyperactive record executive asks as he waggles an action figure in the face of the rapper Common in a comic scene from the launch commercial for Coca-Cola Classic's "Real" campaign. This record executive, who also makes appearances in skits on two Eminem CDs (in one he's shot to death by the rapper, who mistakenly believes that the executive is about to insult his new album), is one of the few corporate suits who is engaging enough as an actor that he could give up his day job. Except for this: He is very good at his day job.

Meet Steve Berman, a ball of energy who is universally described as one of the smartest marketing minds in the music business. Berman runs marketing for Interscope/Geffen/A&M, the Universal Music

Group labels overseen by Jimmy Iovine. That gives him a leg up to begin with, since Iovine is one of the most powerful players in the music business.

Berman's musical roots run deep. His grandfather, Sy Waronker, was a studio musician who cofounded Liberty Records in the 1950s. An uncle was an executive at Warner Records, where Berman started work in the mailroom in the early 1980s. He hooked up with Iovine about a decade later and has been a key player on his team since then. He's also one of the more vocal advocates of the intersection of music and advertising.

Interscope completed one of the biggest such deals when it linked with Coca-Cola and ad agency Berlin Cameron/Red Cell on a Coke Classic ad campaign for which Common and the singer Mya recorded a song, "Real compared to what?" They performed this song in the commercials, and it later appeared as a track on Mya's debut album.

"We went to Mya and Common not with a product endorsement, but with an idea that would give them exposure while giving Coca-Cola something that would be at the core of its message," said Berman. "From our perspective, it's not a commercial; it's a record and a visual interpretation of that message.

"Music is more popular than ever. If you tap into a culture, the market is still there, but figuring out how to monetize that is difficult in a world where CD sales have shrunk 20 percent," Berman went on. "We've decided to work with strong brands where we're targeting a similar audience."

Berman believes that such alliances can be win-win, marrying the bigger budgets of marketers with the youth-lifestyle expertise of music labels: "Together, we can penetrate into the consumer and make stuff happen."

Like many players in the Madison & Vine space, Berman believes that the "accident that caused this whole thing" was a director's inclusion of a Jaguar in the video for a Sting single, "Desert Rose" (a deal that is explored extensively in the next chapter). Although that alliance was far from the first link between the music and ad businesses, it is widely considered to have been a seminal moment, moving such partnerships well beyond corporate sponsorship of a concert tour or advertisers' licensing of old hits for use in commercials. The Sting deal sparked a new wave of collaborations that serve the needs of both advertisers and the creators and sellers of recorded and live music.

A veritable laundry list of deals have followed on the heels of this one. As freelance writer Marc Pollack wrote in *Advertising Age* in July 2003, "Advertising has become the music industry's new favorite suitor." Consider these examples:

> The R&B singer Mary J. Blige appeared in a commercial for sneaker maker Reebok and the Lady Foot Locker chain of stores that was designed to look like a music video. The Reebok tie-in also included the creation of a Mary J. Blige clothing line and sponsorship of her next tour.

> Chrysler Group inked a 3-year, $14 million pact
> to have the singer Celine Dion promote its
> line of vehicles in songs and through
> appearances in commercials. The automaker
> also sponsored the singer's appearances in
> Las Vegas.
>
> McDonald's signed boy-band heartthrob Justin
> Timberlake to pen an original tune, "I'm
> lovin' it," which was used as the tag line in a
> global ad campaign for the fast-food
> company. The former member of 'NSync
> appeared in the kickoff commercial and also
> made promotional appearances on behalf of
> the burger chain.

These music tie-ins are perhaps more valuable to new artists than to established ones, giving them an opportunity to break through when they can't get radio play or marketing support for their music. Mitsubishi Motors, for example, has a long-running ad campaign that features young people grooving to music as they tool around town in their cars. The songs in the ads are often from obscure, forgotten, or as-yet-undiscovered artists (Dirty Vegas and Nick Drake are two examples). Soon after new commercials run, Mitsubishi is besieged by requests for information about the music, and the songs quickly become popular files on download sites. The carmaker has even considered selling CDs filled with songs from its ads.

The deals don't always work out smoothly. Chrysler's use of Celine Dion to sell minivans and other family vehicles was widely ridiculed by many in the advertising business, who saw a poor fit between the singer and the brand and doubted that the Canadian chanteuse would drive herself anywhere instead of being driven around in the back of a limousine.

The early ads also came under fire from Chrysler dealers because they focused more on the singer than on the product and did little to "move metal," in auto industry lingo. "They show a commercial on TV with Celine Dion going down the road in a [Chrysler] Crossfire and they never even talk about the car," said one Chrysler dealer. "Instead of showing [Celine] in a car, show her putting a stroller in the back of a Pacifica and loading up all her kids in the car so people can see what you can do with the car." Critics charged that the commercials were better at selling CDs than at selling Chryslers.

Chrysler publicly supported Dion, but it began to scale back her role in its ads and to speak only in vague terms about how it would use her in the future. Tom Marinelli, executive vice president in charge of marketing for Chrysler, said that while Celine Dion's association with the brand would continue, "We [need to] make sure, particularly when we are launching a new product, that cars are the stars and she doesn't overwhelm." Chrysler ultimately parted ways with the agency that introduced the carmaker to Dion.

The key to success is the need for advertisers and music labels to respect each other's role. Too often, observers say, there's a danger that one partner will see its role as more important and lose respect for what the other side brings to the table.

"The problem sometimes is, the music industry and certainly the record company [think] we are the center of the universe, so everybody wants us," said one music industry executive. "We have to give something back. That's going to be the real learning curve."

Interscope's Jimmy Iovine has formed collaborations with a number of marketers, but he displayed some of that sense of entitlement when he talked about advertiser tie-ins, presenting them not so much in terms of how marketers might help the music business, but rather in terms of why record labels deserve more money from advertisers or film studios or MTV—any partner that makes money off of music.

"When you create popular culture, you should benefit by it," Iovine said. "MTV is more valuable right now than every record company combined. Its valuation is larger than all five major record companies. We will start to pick up revenues from the coattail that we create. If we're involved in creating popular culture, whether it be [the Eminem film] *Eight Mile* or a deal we have with a soft drink company, we're going to be paid around our music. The other people are."

CAA's Rob Light sees a different business model, one in which advertisers could get a cut of music sales, giving them an incentive to promote the artists and labels they work with more heavily.

> Why doesn't a label call an advertiser and say, "Look, we're going to give you two points on every record we sell, and we want you to use only our music," and give them an incentive to be involved and promote

their records as their records are promoting that brand? No one's ever said to an advertiser, "Hey! You can be a participant." Somewhere in the future, that's going to happen, as brands become more conscious of their dollars.

Light also believes that music tie-ins will get much deeper than the use of original and licensed music in commercials, and tour sponsorships. One idea he has is for an advertiser to put up a couple of hundred thousand dollars, a small investment, to buy vans that it could paint with a brand message and then give to 10 new bands to take out on the road. That will take a new, longer-term mindset concerning how such investments are viewed. It's more about changing or reinforcing a brand image over time than it is about immediate sales gains.

"You're not going to feel the impact of that two weeks later in a 7-Eleven," Light said. "But over the course of a year, the consciousness that this brand is embracing new music and embracing the lifestyle of these kids will be felt. A whole new generation of marketers and a whole new generation of musicians are going to find ways to work together."

Ken Hertz is a senior partner in the law firm Goldring Hertz & Lichtenstein who specializes in the music business and represents such artists as Will Smith and Alannis Morisette. He is also a big believer in such collaborations and has put together Membrain, an entertainment marketing consulting group in the space:

Record companies are saying, hey, we have these exclusive rights, exclusive relationships with artists; let's figure out other ways to make money on this. But the problem is that they're not very good marketers, and because they weren't good at marketing the product, they have very low batting averages, but they owned the distribution channel. That has now, you know, gone away. What they've now sort of clued into is the idea that entertainment content is a great way to leverage audience affinity for an artist into an affinity for another brand.

Chapter 14

Driving Miles

The pop singer Sting, clad all in black leather and looking impossibly cool, is performing at a nightclub as impossibly beautiful women writhe to the beat of his ballad. "Everyone dreams of becoming a rock star," the on-screen type reads, before asking, "What then do rock stars dream of?" The answer comes as a shot of Sting, with his eyes closed, switches to one of him riding in the back seat of a sleek black Jaguar speeding along the Las Vegas strip.

Is this a video for Sting's Middle Eastern–tinged single "Desert Rose" or a commercial for Jaguar? Yes.

It's both, and it's a lot more than that.

A year can be an eternity in the what-have-you-done-for-me-lately culture of Hollywood. But several years after it was done, entertainment and music executives still speak in reverent tones when they

discuss the Sting-Jaguar deal of 2000, a unique partnership that caused sales of both $50,000 cars and
$20 CDs to soar.

It's a touchstone, one that's particularly relevant
as music labels aggressively combat the piracy that they
blame for decimating sales of recorded music.

It's impossible to explore how the music business
might align itself with the advertising business without
exploring the Sting-Jaguar alliance. With that in mind,
I visited the architect of that deal at his home office in
West Hollywood. The alliance would never have
happened, everyone involved agrees, had it not been for
Miles Axe Copeland III, then Sting's manager.

"Miles's things were very, very important to
what's happening in music today," says Jimmy Iovine,
the president of music labels Interscope/Geffen/A&M.
"Because he took an artist with the credibility of Sting
and took a gigantic step forward. And a lot of what
you're seeing right now is because of Sting and Jaguar
and Miles. We learned a lot from them."

"They were the first ones," agrees Steve Berman,
who runs the marketing operations at Iovine's labels.
"Miles saw the art, the video, was not representative of
Sting in a negative way. It was truly Sting represented
as Sting is. And Miles drove the thing completely. He
reached out to [ad agency] Ogilvy, he reached out to
Jaguar, he came back with the deal on the table."

Miles Copeland's connection to the music business and his relationship with the singer went back
many years. His brother Stewart was the drummer in
the popular 1980s band The Police, fronted by Sting,
and Miles was the band's manager. When Sting decided

in 1984 to pursue a solo career, Miles continued as his manager.

Copeland is soft-spoken but passionate and prone to bouts of shouting when he warms up to his topic. He runs a specialty music label, Ark 21, that markets world music, including the work of artists from Latin America and the Middle East. (Copeland's father was a CIA operative, and young Miles was raised in places such as Syria, Egypt, and Lebanon.) Ark 21 has its headquarters in a modest pink stucco building behind Copeland's home in West Hollywood. The entrance, through a locked fence at the top of a dead-end street, is unmarked. On the day I visited, I rang a bell outside the fence, and a young, casually dressed man skipped down the backyard stairs to greet me. "This is the right place," he said, before I even asked. Copeland appeared out of a back office moments later, and we retreated to a small, private courtyard between his home and his office.

I asked Miles to tell me the story behind the Jaguar deal, in his own words, and to share his views on the future of the music business. He is definitely not shy about his role; his bio on the Ark 21 Web site notes that he "unwittingly virtually revolutionized the use of corporate advertising" to market music.

The story begins with the video shoot for "Desert Rose," the second single from Sting's late 1999 album *Brand New Day*. The script called for Sting to be driven through the desert to a nightclub. Director Paul Boyd chose a Jaguar S-Type, seeing it as a cool, contemporary vehicle that at the same time evoked a classic elegance.

Copeland had wanted to go with "Desert Rose" as the first radio single to promote the new album, but he was overruled by record company executives, who thought the song, which begins not with Sting's voice but with that of an Algerian singer (Cheb Mami, chanting in Arabic), was too exotic. "The radio people said it would never get played. I was told if you want to have a chance with this song in America, you've got to take the Arab guy off of it."

The decision was made to release "Brand New Day" first instead. But the single wasn't able to get radio time. Copeland said it aired on only 10 "Top 40" stations across the country. That didn't bode well for the new album.

The "Desert Rose" video, shot outside of Las Vegas, changed everything. When Copeland saw the finished video, he says, he realized, "My God, it's a car commercial we've made. Literally. The car was as much a feature as Sting was."

He contacted a friend who worked for an advertising agency and asked which agency handled the Jaguar account. The answer came back: Ogilvy & Mather in New York, an American agency owned by a British holding company called WPP Group.

"So I call them up, and I say, 'Hey, my name's Miles Copeland, I manage Sting, and as a courtesy call, we've made an ad for your Jaguar, using Sting's music and Sting's in it; I hope you don't mind, and I'm going to send you the video.' And he's on the other end of the phone, going, 'Excuse me? You did what?'"

Copeland sent a copy of the video to the agency's New York office and said he got a call back within days expressing interest. But if Ogilvy & Mather was intrigued by the video, the agency was even more stunned by Copeland's proposal: "'If you will make the commercial look like an ad for my record, I'll give you the rights for free. Just as long as you have a big enough TV campaign to make this worthwhile.' For me to go in there and get a million here and a million there, that wasn't what the game was. I wanted the money on the screen, on TV, that's where I needed the money."

The label had earmarked $1.8 million to market the album, Copeland said, including $800,000 to produce music videos. By contrast, Jaguar had a U.S. advertising budget of $18.9 million and a strategy that included heavy use of TV advertising. Copeland's blue eyes still sparkle when he recalls the figures, almost unheard of in music marketing.

The finished Jaguar commercial went well beyond anything that had been seen before in terms of promoting Sting's album. The artist and his song weren't relegated to the background, nor did music credits appear in unreadable small type along the bottom of the screen. Instead, just seconds after the commercial begins, the screen goes black and these words appear in silver type: "Sting/Desert Rose/From the Album Brand New Day." The Jaguar name isn't mentioned or displayed on the screen until the closing seconds of the spot. "There's no question it's a commercial for my product," Copeland says. "It's a Sting ad." (Of course, many artists lack the clout of Sting and could never demand such clear credit in an ad, leaving it to interested viewers to dig out the information, often on the Internet, about the artist and the song they heard in the ad.)

Before the commercial aired, Sting had gotten very little radio play for the exotic single—"We had zero Top 40 stations," Copeland says—and U.S. sales ambitions for the album were a modest 1 million. But after the ad hit the airwaves, fans deluged radio stations with requests for the song. Copeland says that "Desert Rose" ultimately played on 180 Top 40 stations, and sales soared. It was Sting's biggest single in more than a decade and the best-selling solo album of his career, selling 4 million copies in the United States and another 4 million around the world. Jaguar S-Type sales also quadrupled as younger buyers flocked to dealers, lowering the median age of owners of the luxury vehicles, an important goal for the automaker.

The deal was a watershed, Copeland says, because, while classic hits had long been licensed for commercials, "This was the first time it was an unknown song by a contemporary artist." Ultimately, he believes, "the reason it worked was that it was . . . a natural association, and both products looked good. It was a win for everybody."

> The art of linking the people together is to understand what each has to benefit . . . how each has to benefit, and the fact that if both parties benefit, it's a double effect, because as Sting got bigger, so did the power of the Jaguar commercial.

Copeland believes that there are other lessons that can be learned from the alliance, and that it can serve as a model for the music industry.

Could it be done again? Absolutely. But it has to work equally for both parties. The problem with the advertisers comes when it's weighted to the person laying out the money. They're cutting a check, they're making the commercial, they're laying out a lot of money, they're going to call the shots; it weights their way. That is the mistake that most of these things make. They don't get the impact because they buy the talent. But because it's obvious they bought it, it diminishes the value of that talent. So they've effectively undermined their purchase.

Music labels, he believes, make a different mistake by wanting to take money from advertisers without ceding any creative control.

Copeland scoffs at the idea that artists who do deals with marketers will be accused of selling out and will lose credibility with their fans.

Sting didn't have to get away with it, because the public never cared. All this old view that somehow it destroys your credibility turns out to be a load of hogwash. The public doesn't care. The reality is, Bruce Springsteen could do a big commercial and as long as it was tasteful and it was cool and the product was okay, nobody would really care, except for a few precious people who probably wouldn't buy the record anyway.

Perhaps proving the point, one of rock's most prominent advertising holdouts, Bob Dylan, appeared in a commercial for Victoria's Secret in spring 2004 that caused barely a stir among critics or his fan base.

Entertainment attorney Ken Hertz agrees.

There's a broader range of what you're defining as talent than there used to be. Artists fought really, really hard in the 1970s to avoid having their records look like an advertising medium. Because the artist's relationship with its audience is fragile, right? The difference now is that a lot of art still populates the shelves in a record store, but a lot of stuff that can't fairly be described as art but has to be described as commercial content is far less precious about it. What is New Kids On the Block? What is Backstreet Boys? What is this sort of manufactured content which is designed to appeal to an audience that doesn't really relate to a collaborative work, where the artist didn't write the song, the artist didn't produce the track, the artist didn't play the instruments.

In any case, those involved may not have a choice. "We all need to spread the risk and to get help," Copeland said.

The record business cannot afford to take the burden of breaking a record and [an] artist all on its own, particularly with all the other stuff that's going on. Everybody is being forced to [look] at how they can spread their risk and get more contributors into making something happen, because the labels absolutely are not in the position they were 3 years ago. And the position is worsening, not getting better.

It will never be the same again. If in effect the public eventually buys its music digitally, paying 99 cents a song, that will mean there will still be a vibrant business, but instead of being album business, it will be song business; we'll go back to the days when the single was the basic core of the business, which means that the amount of money will decrease overall. Which puts more and more pressure on the labels. It still costs a lot of money to break a single. That's not going to change. Only now you can't sell albums off of it.

So it's all the more reason to link up with advertisers. The union between the advertiser and the music people is going to be greater and greater.

Chapter 15

Crossing the Line

In discussions about content-commerce alliances, a great deal of attention is typically given to doing deals that meet the objectives of both sides—the marketer and the entertainment company. Too often, what is not mentioned is the most important party in the transaction: the consumer.

In the spring of 2002, I wrote a column that was interpreted by some people as a signal that I didn't believe in the Madison & Vine phenomenon. That, however, wasn't the point of the piece. Rather, it was intended as a warning: If you forget to keep the consumer at the center of everything, you will blow this opportunity.

The business of advertising-supported media has always operated with a fairly simple model. Content creators (whether TV programmers, magazine editors, or filmmakers) create products that they believe will appeal to a certain segment of the population. If they are right, they will obtain an audience that has something of a bond with those products—a viewer who is loyal to a television program, a newspaper reader who trusts the editorial page of her local daily. Advertisers then buy time or space in those products to leverage that relationship by association. The loyal reader of *GQ* is probably predisposed to think that any fashion designer who advertises in the publication has met a certain quality standard.

But in the convergence of Madison Avenue and Hollywood, there is a very real danger that content will be developed first and foremost with an advertiser's needs in mind, and will only then seek an audience. Many marketers' motivation for gaining creative input into story lines and media content is not to have a more engaging dialogue with consumers. Instead, they are motivated by the fear that DVRs will make 30-second ads obsolete. How do you connect to consumers who can give you a brusque technological brush-off?

Forgetting that the consumer comes first is a sure-fire model for disaster, one that leads to weak products that are unable to attract an audience, or earn its trust if they do attract it. The public loses out. The media company loses out. The advertiser loses out.

The other concern is that the new forms of advertising through entertainment will be executed lazily and without imagination, and thus will become little more than a return to the product placements and title sponsorships of the early days of radio and television. This would amount to responding to one of the most revolutionary technological challenges in decades with a half-hearted, warmed-over solution.

TV networks have embraced product integration not to satisfy viewer demand, but because the escalation of production costs has destroyed their economic model. Poorly done, product integration is dangerous because of the real risk that it will damage the consumer's relationship with both the advertiser and the media outlet. When done right, however, product integration can enhance both a brand's image and the entertainment experience. In the best cases, the product is a comfortable fit with the content, and perhaps even provides a measure of verisimilitude. (Stephen King novels are certainly scarier because his characters live in the same world as the rest of us—they drive Chevrolets and guzzle Cokes. I approached King at the National Book Awards, where he was being honored with a lifetime achievement award, and asked him whether he had done this purposely. "It's not something I was ever conscious of," he said. "The one thing I did know was that when you open your medicine cabinet at home, you don't see Brand X.")

But bad product-integration deals are clunky and unnatural, and are often rejected by consumers—who then lose their trust in the advertisers and the media company that present them with such transparent dreck.

Consumers will reject poor attempts to disguise commercials as entertainment. When in 2002 Ford Motor Company signed a deal with NBC's *Tonight Show* to sponsor concerts on the program, the *Wall Street Journal* reported Ford's plan to fill the stage with

Lincolns, then noted, "Lincoln also would like to have the musical performers be driven onto the stage in Lincoln vehicles." How's that for seamless, natural integration? "Why not go the next step?" I wrote in a column critical of the deal. "Have Jay Leno deliver his monologue on the hood of a Lincoln and interview guests from the front seat. The blatant disregard for the viewer is almost staggering."

Ellis Verdi of DeVito/Verdi warned in the *Journal* of the danger of overstepping the bounds: "You cheapen the product." He didn't specify whether his reference was to the media product or the advertised product, but the warning applies to both.

There are other examples of wrongheaded entertainment alliances. CBS today is one of the most forward-thinking networks in doing product integration deals, and its use of such tie-ins in the reality show *Survivor* has been applauded by many people in the space. The Tiffany Network wasn't always so astute, however.

In 1996, CBS staged a promotional stunt to boost sales of Elizabeth Taylor's Black Pearls perfume. La Liz appeared in four of the network's sitcoms on a Monday night during the February sweeps period, when networks are shooting for their highest ratings. The common story line that ran through the plots of all the programs was the actress's search for a missing string of black pearls. Get it?

It was a crass placement that seemed to signal that CBS was more interested in keeping advertisers happy than in entertaining its viewers. The issue surfaced again 3 years later, when CBS decided to sell replicas of the jewelry worn by characters on the soap opera *Guiding Light*. Once again, profitability trumped credibility.

CBS instructed the soap's writers to weave the product directly into the plot of the show so that it could sell lots of $29.95 baubles. That corrupted the creative process; instead of the writers' goal being to entertain viewers, their goal was to make more money for the network. Defenders of CBS countered that the jewelry promotion was a solid example of the marriage of content and commerce. Let's hope not. If all the grand theories of convergence truly boil down to a world in which viewers can buy replicas of the jewelry worn by the characters in a soap opera, a lot of intellectual and financial resources are being misspent.

In 2000, it was ABC that crossed the line. Its morning talk show *The View*, which was produced by the entertainment division but featured journalists such as the venerable Barbara Walters, cut a deal with Campbell Soup Company that gave the product a starring role in the show. In one program, Walters talked about eating Campbell Soup as a child while her co-hosts hummed the brand's "M'm! M'm! Good!" tag line. ABC and Walters defended the marketing deal and said that it didn't affect the show's quality. Exposing their hypocrisy, however, they then killed a planned segment in which another host was scheduled to roam the studio testing the audience's soup-sipping abilities. (You can't make this stuff up.)

Such deals show a complete lack of imagination and forward thinking. They treat viewers as morons while betraying their trust. A brand boils down to a promise to the consumer to deliver a product or service at a consistent quality. If Campbell were to put inferior soup in a red-and-white can to bolster its bottom line, it would betray that promise. When *The View* put together an inferior entertainment product designed with a marketer rather than a viewer in mind, it did the same thing.

Product placement may seem like an effective marketing tool, but it's a poor substitute for an idea.

In 2003, I again stirred up this debate with a column critical of a much-hyped NBC reality program called *The Restaurant*. The show was already a rather unusual collaboration between Reveille, a production company headed by Ben Silverman, a former William Morris agent turned reality-show producer; Mark Burnett, the visionary (and extremely sponsor-friendly) producer behind the reality hits *Survivor* and *The Apprentice*; and Magna Global Entertainment, one of the world's largest media-buying agencies. The product placement deals put in place with Magna Global clients covered the cost of producing the show, leaving NBC little risk in airing it.

But the so-called mini-commercials in the show for participating brands seemed to break the cardinal rule of product integration: Make it seamless and subtle. "Anyone interested in the brand integration space" needed to study *The Restaurant*, I wrote, "to learn what absolutely not to do."

Already a dreadful show on its own, *The Restaurant* was rendered nearly unwatchable by product placements that were aggressive, intrusive, and clunky—anything but the seamless blend that is necessary to make them bearable, never mind bringing them near to the (perhaps unattainable) standard of enhancing the programming.

The Restaurant, which chronicled the opening of an upscale New York Italian restaurant by celebrity chef Rocco DiSpirito, was not content with showing American Express cards being used to pay for meals and Coors beer being served to customers along with other drinks, or shots of Rocco pulling up to the door in his Mitsubishi (all tie-in partners). Instead, it repeatedly and blatantly crossed the line and tested the limits of viewers' tolerance.

In the first episode, Rocco pulled up in his SUV in front of hundreds of hopefuls auditioning for jobs as waiters and bartenders. One young guy at the front of the line turned to another and said something like (and this was supposedly spontaneous, even though he was wearing a microphone), "What a perfect car for Rocco. What a chick-mobile." In another episode, a weary Rocco reviewed the restaurant's financials after a particularly draining day. He was slumped in a chair, fretting that more money was going out than coming in, when he suddenly announced to the camera, "I know what I'll do. I'll have Stacy apply for a line of credit from American Express's Open: The Small Business Network." The camera then cut to a shot of his assistant at AmEx's Open Web site.

The placement appeared crass and phony, making it difficult to enjoy or trust the show. The American Express Open ads featuring Rocco that appeared during almost every commercial break rubbed salt in the wound.

The Restaurant was not the only show to cross the line, but it demonstrated vividly what can go wrong in the brand-integration space: how fragile the connection with an audience can be, and the cost if it's lost. (That said, NBC and the producers and sponsors of *The Restaurant* claimed to be happy with its ratings performance and even signed on for a second season, although insiders said that the product plugs would be much subtler. John Hayes, global chief marketing officer for American Express, admitted that when he watched one episode at home with his family, the overt product plugs made him cringe. Still, he said the company's research did not turn up widespread audience disapproval.) In this brave new world, the consumers will eventually define the line and won't be afraid to bark at those who cross it.

"You're going to see some shows doing it extremely well, where you're hardly aware that you've been sold something. And then there are going to be some shows where you're going to cringe, where it won't feel right," said CBS Chairman Leslie Moonves. "Hopefully the creators will do it subtly; they will care about their product. If they don't, if it's bothering people, they always have the clicker. They can turn off the show."

Coca-Cola's Steve Heyer believes that true brand integration moves beyond product placement to ideas that feel natural and relevant to the consumer and reflect the brand's positioning. He cited Coca-Cola's Red Room on the reality TV series *American Idol*. The backstage area where contestants gather is decorated Coca-Cola red and includes a Coke vending machine and clock and a red couch with a white Coca-Cola ribbon running along its length.

The key, Heyer said, is to be "critically incidental."

"At a key moment that feels right, the product has to be accepted and feel appropriate. If it's jarring, if it's false, everyone knows that. It's perfectly natural to see a red room behind the scenes of *American Idol*. It ties to a passion—music. It ties to American passions—winning, competition, voyeurism." Coke's goal is to build Red Rooms for other televised events, including one at the Olympics, in the village, where athletes could hang out and chug icy Cokes, preferably on camera.

If that sounds too blatantly commercial, it proves the point that defining the line between appropriate and over the top is a subjective task.

"Organic always has a longer-lasting effect," said one Hollywood veteran. "You can weave it in, in an organic way, and not hit somebody over the head. As corny as this may sound, even with *American Idol*, Coke was organically part of that show. You and I watching it, seeing the red couch and cooler in the back room probably seemed like, 'Man, they're getting hit over the head with a sledgehammer.' But to the kids watching, it was organically part of the show. It was actually a better spot because it didn't feel like it was hitting them over the head."

Good taste also has to come into play. In December 2003, Chrysler Group canceled plans for its Dodge brand to sponsor "Lingerie Bowl 2004," a pay-per-view event that was set to air against the Super Bowl half-time show and to feature models in lingerie playing a game of tackle football. Dodge's involvement was going to include logos on the lingerie and the Dodge name scripted into the show's logo. When it announced the deal, Dodge said that it would attract the brand's "core demographic"—young males. But women's groups and others denounced the show as sexist and exploitative, and Dodge finally pulled out, saying that its sponsorship "has become a distraction" that was "diverting media and consumer attention . . . from the great products we are preparing to launch."

Sometimes, even if you cross the line, you can still cross back.

Chapter 16

The Connectors

When there's a land rush, one thing is certain: Lots of people show up. Some of them are legitimate, some shady, but all of them want to stake their claim. Just such a rush is underway at the intersection of Madison & Vine.

As the Madison & Vine phenomenon surfaced, as a series of seemingly unrelated deals began to converge to form the blurry outlines of a coherent movement, one of the most striking developments was the rapid emergence of new companies, or units of existing companies, that wanted in, that wanted to be among the early explorers of this new space. They wanted, in most cases, riches. In that way, it was more a gold rush than a land rush, with no one being certain whether this new stream that they had stumbled upon held great reserves of wealth or merely a few morsels of fool's gold. Not that this deterred them.

At one point, digital technologies were supposed to mark the end of the intermediary by enabling direct communication and transactions between those who had something to sell and those who wanted to buy. In the late 1990s, the idea was that so-called bricks-and-mortar retailers (known until then simply as stores) were going to be put out of business by the Internet, which would enable manufacturers to sell their products directly to customers. Similarly, there would be no need for intermediaries in almost any transaction. Disintermediation was a big buzzword. That concept, however, was deflated along with the Internet bubble in 2000. And as this space began to emerge, intermediaries seemed poised to play an even larger role in helping anxious studios and marketers, who didn't really know or trust each other, didn't understand each other's business challenges, and often didn't seem to speak the same language, to navigate and chart this brave new world. "Vine looks at Madison as a checkbook," said one savvy Hollywood observer. "Madison looks at Vine with starry eyes, unapproachable."

These intermediaries took many forms. Advertising agencies—which tend to be overly sensitive to any perceived threats to their client relationships—opened up units specializing in entertainment, trying to extend the services they offered advertisers. Hollywood talent agencies, meanwhile, created units specializing in marketing, seeking to sign up marketers who viewed the entertainment business with awe and who feared having their pockets picked if they tried to walk through the town without a street-smart escort.

This put the talent agencies and ad agencies in the uneasy position of having to partner in some situations while in other cases competing to represent an advertiser in the entertainment space. (This wasn't the first time there had been conflict and tension between the two sides. Way back in 1989, Coca-Cola Company shocked both the advertising and entertainment industries when it fired its long-time ad agency and handed the advertising account for its flagship soft drink, Coke, to Creative Artists Agency. Although the talent shop produced some interesting work for Coke early on—becoming best known for commercials showing animated polar bears that loved to guzzle the soda—Coca-Cola eventually returned the business to traditional ad agencies. Still, the move of this business sent shudders through both coasts and left ad agencies and talent agencies distrustful of each other's motives and ambitions.)

The talent and ad shops, however, were far from the only intermediaries—they prefer to be called connectors—crowding the corner of Madison & Vine. Entertainment industry lawyers suddenly and surprisingly became marketing experts. Old-school product-placement firms that specialized in finding props for films reinvented themselves as strategic integration specialists. In addition, new companies were founded specifically to specialize in marketing through entertainment. Their backers were former executives at studios, ad agencies, TV networks, talent shops, and marketers. Some of them wanted to work for the studios, some for ad agencies, some directly with clients. All of them hoped to stake their claim.

Here are two of their stories.

H. Mitchell Kanner

In retrospect, it seems that the career of H. Mitchell Kanner, known to all as Mitch, was headed in the direction of branded entertainment from the outset. But even a few years back, that wouldn't have seemed so obvious.

What was obvious all along was that Kanner was an extraordinary "networker," someone who seemed to know everyone in the business and everything about them and to be adept at connecting various people to others in his network, creating a sphere around himself that was constantly growing and changing shape. Now, the entertainment and advertising businesses are all about relationships, meaning that most people who succeed in them have strong schmoozing skills. They know a lot of people, and they know how to work a cocktail party. Even in those worlds, however, Kanner stood out. For years, he worked at Digital Domain, a digital-effects company best known for the special effects it created for the blockbuster film *Titanic*. Kanner's work with the company was in the area of commercial production, and his main task was to sell Digital Domain's services to ad agencies. In the ad business, he was a highly visible presence, particularly at the annual International Advertising Festival in Cannes, France, which celebrates advertising creativity. There never seemed to be a dinner or a party that Kanner wasn't at the center of, usually surrounded by a laughing group of boldface names. He seemed to know thousands of attendees personally, and in hundreds of cases he knew their spouses as well.

After he left Digital Domain, Kanner reinvented himself as more of a Hollywood player, one of the first to preach the idea that the advertising and entertainment industries needed to work together more closely, as each could plug gaps in the other's business plans. In 2001, he set up a consultancy that worked mostly with ad agencies and the major marketing communications holding companies that owned them, helping them to understand and navigate the entertainment industries. Kanner lived in Los Angeles, but he flew to New York almost weekly, taking advantage of his first-class plane seats and four-star hotel perches to constantly widen his circle of business contacts.

In January 2003, Kanner decided to try to build a real business. He teamed up with two powerful, well-connected Hollywood players to create a new company called Integrated Entertainment Partners. His partners were Rich Frank, the former chairman of Walt Disney Television, and a high-powered entertainment attorney named Skip Brittenham. Also brought on board was a long-time advertising agency executive, Christopher Gebhardt.

Kanner untied himself from the ad agencies he had worked with. Instead, he and his partners wanted to represent studios and networks, to get early information on scripts and development projects. They would then brainstorm on ways to integrate brands and seek out marketers that would fit those projects. They pitched their points of differentiation as access—between them, the partners could in theory get a meeting with everyone who mattered in Hollywood and in the advertising business—and neutrality. "We're like the Swiss," Kanner told *Advertising Age*'s *Madison & Vine* at the time IEP hung out its shingle.

Friends of Kanner and Frank endorsed the company from its start, giving it added credibility. The *Ad Age* story on its launch quoted, among others, Dream-Works founder Jeffrey Katzenberg, who had worked with Frank at Disney; Revolution Studios founder Joe Roth; and Geoffrey Frost, the head of marketing for telecommunications powerhouse Motorola.

IEP's touted neutrality didn't last long, however; in March 2004, the company unveiled a merger with The Firm, a highly regarded Beverly Hills talent management firm. Frank was named chairman of the board of the new company, which kept the Firm name. Firm founder Jeff Kwatinetz retained his role as CEO and co-chairman, a title he shares with partner Rick Yorn. Kanner, who took over the brand marketing practice, told AdAge.com that the merger represented "the nexus of the intersection of talent, creative and strategic marketing expertise."

Kanner said that he first began to draw the parallels between advertising and entertainment in his mind during the making of *Titanic*. Filmmakers and ad agency creatives were both great storytellers, with the former using 2-hour films to tell their stories and the latter using 30- and 60-second commercials. Around the same time, Kanner was doing consulting for the head of a chain of movie theaters, developing ideas on how to get kids into theaters on Saturday mornings, when the theaters usually sat empty. One of Kanner's ideas was to get cereal makers to sponsor the showing of serial films similar to the ones shown in theaters in the 1950s. Instead of popcorn, kids who attended the showings would sample breakfast foods. The concept, Cereal Serials, never took off. But the idea of bringing together consumer brands and entertainment companies had taken root in Kanner's mind, and he began to develop a thesis on the topic.

"It was very clearly about brand integration in content, not about brand-sponsored entertainment," Kanner said. "Brand-sponsored goes back to the 1950s. Brand integration never existed. The reason it exists today isn't because it's any terrific art form or a really smart idea about how to make content more viable or more contextual. It's because there's a problem to solve where brands can't really get share of mind of the consumer."

Kanner explains the difference between brand integration and brand sponsorship by talking about tie-ins that present the values and personalities of a brand rather than just showing a logo.

"Product placement has been a business for 25 or 30 years already, and it's not a business that actually encourages an understanding of consumer brands. [It's about] production issues—'I need 36 cars.' Production doesn't care where [the cars] come from; they just care that on September 9, when they begin production, those 36 cars are sitting there. GM, Chrysler, they really don't care. The film needs to be produced, and cars are important," Kanner said. "When it becomes interesting is when there is actually a fit, as opposed to product placement just addressing a production issue. We live on earth, and on earth today brands exist in the everyday context. There is no such thing as Main Street, USA. There are no general stores, there are no five-and-dimes. There's Duane Reade, there's Sav-On."

Interestingly, despite being someone who is trying to make a business out of forging such partnerships, Kanner admitted that some of the most successful deals have happened almost by mistake, or through a lucky accident (as many in Hollywood do, he noted the use of the Jaguar in the Sting video as a prime example). But he still believes that as the discipline evolves, there will be more sophisticated, strategically sound deals that will produce successful case studies. His definition of success is fairly straightforward: First, he said, it's determined by the audience reach, measured in sales of a CD, ratings of a TV show, or tickets sold to a film; second, and more important, it's determined by whether the advertiser was able to move product off shelves. "Quite frankly," he said, "those are the only two metrics that matter at the end of the day. And I think the latter metric is the only one that's important anyway, and you should be able to lock that information down a bit more specifically."

Kanner believes that entertainment-advertising alliances will be a big part of the solution to the rise of PVR technology, which he thinks will essentially wipe out the 30-second commercial. "Then, advertisers won't be looking for it, they'll be charged with looking for it," he said. "There will be no traditional advertising." That said, he also admitted that "not all content lends itself to integration," meaning that there could be fewer options for marketers in an integrated model than there are in the interruptive one. In the first few months after his company was launched, Kanner said, "We read about 75 scripts, all green-lit by the CEOs of the studios, all viable products. We worked on three, and of them, one really wasn't a candidate. So Madison Avenue and Hollywood have to be really smart about this."

Tera Hanks

Tera Hanks is a walking reminder of how quickly what was once the basic business of product placement has evolved into something more sophisticated and strategic. She's a young executive, yet old enough to have been around when product placement was little more than a way to get props for a film without paying for them.

After graduating from UCLA with a psychology degree, she landed a job in the marketing department of sneaker maker LA Gear. Through that, she met people in the entertainment business and eventually went to work for Cato Johnson, a product-placement agency. "It was all barter then," she said. "There were virtually no fees. I was providing cars to film crews in exchange for potential exposure. There were no guarantees or contracts. The only time deals were bigger was when the company was actually going to do something promotional to support the marketing of the film, but people didn't do that too often."

A year later, she accepted a job at Davie-Brown, a placement firm that specialized in films. Her charge:

to create a television department for two key clients, Pepsi and Reebok. Davie-Brown had been founded by Jim Davie and Brad Brown in 1985 as the Pepsi-Cola Entertainment Group. Roger Enrico, who was president of Pepsi at the time, "was tired of seeing Coke in the movies every time he went," Hanks said. Enrico turned to Davie, a Pepsi executive who had developed the famous "Pepsi Challenge" taste test but was leaving the company to move to Los Angeles. The Pepsi-Cola Entertainment Group worked exclusively for that one client for the first 5 years, then (with Pepsi's blessing; the company remains a core client) it changed its name and offered its expertise to other companies. Reebok signed on in 1990 as the second client; Hanks came on board the same year as the fourth employee (an assistant was the third).

By 2003, Davie-Brown represented 30 clients and was part of a much larger operation, the Omnicom Group, one of the world's biggest marketing communications holding companies. Omnicom is the parent of several of the most powerful and legendary ad agencies, including DDB Worldwide and BBDO, long-time creator of commercials for Pepsi.

Davie-Brown began to move past basic product placement. It formed relationships between the brands it represented and Hollywood celebrities, setting up display areas in its offices where trend-setting stars such as Ben Affleck, Sandra Bullock, and Samuel Jackson could come to "shop" for free sneakers and other products. It even set up a fully stocked bar with stools and couches if they wanted to hang around to socialize. "We had a relationship, and that would lead to us working with them on other projects," said Hanks. "As they'd go on to become producers, it became broader than just giving product away. It's much more strategic."

In the mid-1990s, Pepsi began to push to get more out of its tie-ins than just on-screen exposure of its soda fountains, cans, and billboards. Jim Davie negotiated to get a Pepsi commercial on the home video of the Tom Cruise film *Top Gun*, the first time that had been done. (Hanks proudly points to other firsts, including a tie-in between *Ants* and Pepsi that was the first use of product placement in an animated film and an alliance for *Star Wars: Episode One* that involved three restaurants—Taco Bell, KFC, and Pizza Hut—owned by the same parent company.)

As marketers began to look for new ways to reach consumers and get a better return on their marketing investments, studios also became more sophisticated about drawing up contracts to squeeze more marketing support out of placement programs.

In 1985, Hanks said, Pepsi would provide about 25 cases of soda each week to the film crew during the 3 months or so that it took to film a movie. That product would appear in the film but would also be used as free refreshments for the film crew, saving the producers money.

As product placement began to get more sophisticated, studios sought fees from their tie-in partners. Hanks wouldn't comment on what a company such as Pepsi would pay, but others in the field said that major marketers often operate with a sliding scale, reading scripts and making offers to producers based on the level of involvement and exposure. They might pay $20,000 to have a sign appear in the background. That rises to $30,000 if their product appears in one scene and to $40,000 if the product appears in two scenes and is handled by a principal character. A verbal mention of the brand name is worth another $10,000.

It's not a lot of money for a film that costs tens of millions to produce, but the value of the deals doesn't come from the placement fees; it's at the back end, typically in the form of marketing support to help promote the film and sell tickets. Placement is also evolving into brand integration, which implies that the marketers' products are no longer props, but characters in the film. A company such as Pepsi might place product in 25 or 30 films a year, but in a much smaller number of projects its participation goes deeper. Big films stand to get millions in marketing support. Advertisers that fund production can spend millions more on that.

Four times a year, Davie-Brown executives gather with Pepsi's marketing team to look at opportunities. "We're not just looking at films. We're also looking at television opportunities. We're looking at what's going on in the music industry," said Hanks. "We work with them to lay out the whole list of everything that's out there for the next 18 months and then identify where the best opportunities are based on the timing, the budgets, and the brand. It is very strategic."

Davie-Brown is aware that in some Hollywood circles, it is still considered basically a prop shop. But Hanks is out to change that view by positioning her company as a much more strategic partner for marketers. (That said, Davie-Brown still provides all the props for Pepsi, such as old-fashioned fountain handles, glasses, and signs, which are stored in a warehouse just yards from Hanks's office.)

"I'm thrilled about the potential and where the business is going, and the fact that entertainment marketing is a much more important part of the overall marketing mix," Hanks said. "We're playing a much more strategic role. It used to be more of a tactical execution role. Now we're working with our clients' media teams, taking a look at the media budget, how do we leverage what's being spent at the networks. We're having those dialogues, which was never the case a few years ago. What a client is asking for is different; it's how can entertainment be used as a communications platform."

Another major change, she said, is how much earlier in the process studios are seeking marketing partners. "A few years ago," she said, "we would look at all the intellectual properties based on what already had distribution. We didn't know what was on someone's development plate. Now producers want to share content that's in development to see whether we can actually affect true integration."

That's because these producers see the potential for tapping a new source of revenue, even if actual spending by marketers on such programs is still relatively limited. In some cases, Hanks said, network license fees fall short of covering production costs, and tie-ins with marketers are a way to both cover that deficit and get help in marketing a show to lure viewers. If, in exchange for that, the marketer gets category exclusivity as an advertiser on the show and brand integration into the programming, the trade-off seems fair to both sides.

Advertisers, though, particularly public companies, have to be cautious about taking ownership positions in programming. They also have to figure out which pool of money to draw from when doing such deals. Typically, that money comes from some mix of research and development, media, and promotion budgets. As such programs become more commonplace, more marketers are likely to create specific budgets for integration.

As for proving the return on that investment, Hanks admitted that there aren't adequate measurement tools yet. "There's really no good quantifiable or qualitative research out there to help support or tap the effectiveness of these programs," she said. "We're trying, first of all, to figure out what we're trying for. Is it brand awareness? Is it a change in the perception of the brand and increases in intent to purchase? Is it tied directly to sales?"

Davie-Brown's goal is to form a consortium of companies, including researchers and clients, to identify what it is they want to measure and then try to develop appropriate measurement tools. Hanks believes, that once marketers have the tools to prove that such investments are worthwhile, more of them will commit to the space.

There's a very, very viable business there. We've talked to all of our clients about how they need to reach consumers, how they have to establish loyalty to the brands. They have to establish an emotional connection, and entertainment and music are the best ways to do that. Campbell Soup wants to become more culturally relevant through entertainment. We get phone calls every day. We're meeting with Banana Republic and the Gap. They want to find out where they can be more integrative to content. The list goes on and on.

As for the tensions inherent in the relationship between Madison Avenue and Hollywood, Hanks believes they are a natural part of the process—one that increases the need for connectors. "Every deal we've ever done is painstaking, because we're in the middle and you're talking two completely different languages. And so I thought, we're the translator through it all. There are very different needs and agendas on both sides. But I don't think there's any more or less tension. It's just that it's two very different businesses trying to come together to create a win-win situation."

Chapter 17

Proof Positive

As with many new media, accountability will be the key to the credibility of branded entertainment alliances. The challenge will be to figure out how to prove the return on investment, to prove that such deals work, while still encouraging advertisers to experiment with new forms of marketing.

British adman John Hegarty's advice to advertisers has been to forget ROI in the early days of this new discipline and take a leap of faith. His goal is to move them past the fear factor that prevents some marketers from exploring the space. But that approach also contributes to the idea that branded entertainment should be kept in a separate box and judged by different standards from other forms of media advertising and marketing. If that happens, it gives marketers an excuse not to carve out a true budget for such initiatives, keeping Madison & Vine deals on the sidelines.

I would argue the opposite, that advertisers must demand that measurement standards be developed to determine the return on Madison & Vine investments, eliminating the easy out. Any Internet media outlet that has fought for what it considers its fair share of advertising budgets understands how the lack of such standards can impede a medium's development.

While there is not as yet an agreed-upon currency system for branded entertainment, there have been several early attempts to attach value to the deals, at least in the television space. Among the more credible entrants is Nielsen Media Research, the standard system for TV ratings, which planned to introduce a program to track product placement ratings for the six major broadcast networks (ABC, CBS, NBC, Fox, WB, and UPN) in 2004.

Measurement standards will also make it easier for networks to put price tags on such deals. Prices for marketer-entertainment alliances tend to vary wildly. In some cases, TV producers want millions of dollars from participating brands; in others, TV network sales forces throw in product placement as a free "added value" element of a larger ad buy.

All of this comes at a time when marketing executives overall, and particularly those at publicly held companies, are being held more accountable for proving the effectiveness of their expenditures, lending an urgency to the need to develop standards.

iTVX was one of the early players in this space, offering marketers such as Kraft Foods, Unilever, and Verizon a service for valuing product placement deals.

Its valuations are based on such factors as how long a product logo appears on the screen, which characters it's handled by, whether it's mentioned by name, and whether it is central to the plot. A Unilever executive told *Television Week* magazine in 2002 that the valuation scale "is going to mean a lot to our organization in terms of putting a value on product placement. It puts a number on it, and people like to see numbers."

Frank Zazza, the founder of iTVX, has said that his goal is to bring hard data to what had been a subjective marketing discipline. Early examples of how the company valued placements ranged from just over $3000 for a three-second background appearance by All detergent in the HBO series *Sex and the City* to more than $200,000 for a more prominent placement of Snuggle in an episode of NBC's *Friends* in which the detergent was mentioned by name by one of the leading characters.

In the fall of 2003, a commercial-ratings service called Intermedia Advertising Group, or IAG, jumped into the fray with its own product to measure the effectiveness of product placements. Its early clients included American Express and Ford.

Philip Guarascio, an IAG board member and former head of marketing for the largest advertiser in the United States, General Motors, told *Ad Age* at the time that, "There is a range of marketers that could benefit from marketing through entertainment but don't have budget flexibility and can't afford to take risks. They might be more willing to try it if there was a better process to evaluate it."

IAG's In-Program Performance service uses a panel of consumers who respond to online surveys designed to measure their recall of and reaction to product placements and sponsored programming. IAG also marries those data with similar information about advertisers' 30-second commercials to help marketers determine how the two work together to affect viewers' product perceptions. IAG CEO Alan Gould's goal is to help the industry develop a pricing model based on the service's measurements.

But Davie-Brown's Tera Hanks cautioned that it was likely that only one of the rival services would ultimately become the primary currency system. "It's critical for the industry that there emerges an industrywide, accepted standard of measurement," she said.

Ultimately, the true measure of whether any marketing expenditure is worth the investment is whether it causes the cash register to ring, in the industry's words—whether sales rise as a result. But that's a brass ring that the ad industry may never actually be able to grasp, as it is extraordinarily difficult to separate the role of advertising from the hundreds of other factors—including price, packaging, and display—that go into consumer decision making. In the early twentieth century, the department store magnate John Wanamaker is supposed to have famously said, "I know I waste half the money I spend on advertising. I just don't know which half." Judging by the industry's continued fascination with that statement even today (during a panel on accountability that I monitored in front of an audience of advertisers, half a dozen people sent questions to the podium asking the panelists whether they had figured out which half), it's a question that has yet to be answered.

Chapter 18

Six Simple Rules

In reading the previous pages, some common themes begin to emerge, threads that wind their way through the various anecdotes, stories, and insights. They can be woven into six quick rules that will serve as guidelines for the development of the Madison & Vine space.

Here are those rules.

1. Reject the Status Quo

This sounds simple, but in industries that are bound by tradition and reliant on entrenched business practices, change is too often avoided, viewed as a messy, chaotic process with no clear outcome. But change is no longer an option; it's an economic necessity. Some will view that reality with fear; others will see opportunity in it and will move to pioneer new forms of marketing. The latter are most likely to emerge as leaders as their industries are redefined.

2. Collaborate

Hollywood is probably better equipped for this than Madison Avenue. Movie studios, talent agents, and other entertainment industry players know well what it's like to work in a town where one day you compete and the next day you collaborate. Studios often share the risks of financing, distributing, and marketing certain films even while they are trying fiercely to steal market share from one another with their other releases. Ad agencies and other marketing services companies are learning how to do that, since many of them are now sibling units of large holding companies. They share some clients but face off in reviews to work for others. Martin Sorrell, chief executive of WPP Group, one of the world's largest marketing communications holding companies, even has a term for it: "kiss and punch." Still, agencies historically are territorial and silo-oriented, and they tend to react poorly to perceived threats to their strangleholds on clients. But it's clear that for branded entertainment programs to succeed, it will take cooperation and coordination from both Madison and Vine. As marketers begin to invest serious dollars in such ventures, they will insist that the various players work together to make deals happen. Those players include TV networks, movie studios, music labels, ad agencies, event organizers, entertainment marketing firms, and public-relations agencies. Putting aside their egos and working together for a common cause is a skill that all sides need to acquire and hone—fast. Those who try to control the process or refuse to work with others—who, in short, see it as Madison vs. Vine—are likely to find themselves sidelined.

3. Demand Accountability

The absence of standards—in measurement, pricing, even definitions—will be the highest hurdle to marketers' acceptance of branded entertainment as a legitimate marketing tool, providing them with an excuse. No one is likely to divert dollars from other media or marketing disciplines with proven track records until it is possible to properly value such deals and determine the return on investment.

In the television space, several companies already offer basic services that try to put a value on product placements. But more complex measurements will be needed, and marketers will also need legitimate benchmarks and standards to determine the success of their film and music alliances. Many entertainment industry experts point out that the measurement tools used to determine the effectiveness and efficiency of traditional advertising buys have serious deficiencies, and many marketers would agree. Still, those tools are accepted currencies in the marketing business, and without similar tools, branded entertainment will continue to be treated more as a space in which to experiment than as a legitimate contender for a notable portion of marketing budgets.

4. Stay Flexible

The business of branded entertainment is truly in its infancy. The only certainty is that it will change and evolve, and a few years from now it will probably look very different from the way it looks today. What's indisputable is that digital technologies have shifted the power from the creators of content to the consumers of it, and that this will force changes in how marketers and entertainment providers communicate with their audiences. As with the emergence of interactive media, solutions will take many forms, ranging from basic product placement to content ownership to forms of interactive advertising that have yet to be envisioned. It's important for marketers to experiment with various things and not to wed themselves to one model. As the Madison & Vine space evolves into new forms, marketers must be willing to change as well.

5. Let Go

In an intrusive advertising environment, marketers were able to maintain total control over the message they put in front of consumers. But as they cede control to their audiences and collaborate with content creators, they will have to learn to loosen their grip on their brands, even to let their consumers define what those brands stand for.

Had BMW refused to allow a character in one of its films to bleed to death in the back seat of a Beemer, the carmaker wouldn't have been able to hire the top directors in Hollywood and could never have earned credibility with viewers.

This is likely to be one of the most frightening prospects faced by marketers. It can be extremely uncomfortable, for example, for a brand manager to listen as a character in a sitcom makes a joke at the expense of his product. And there can be a danger in going too far in allowing consumers to define brands if their definition strays too far from the marketer's. But advertisers take just as great a risk if they insist on giving content creators thick books of rules on how their brands and brand icons can and can't appear in scripts. As Stephen King said, real brands exist in the real world, and the real world is a complex space.

Those marketers that are able to let go, are able to laugh at themselves, are likely to be surprised by how much respect and loyalty they earn from consumers.

Speaking of which, the first five rules ultimately lead to the most important one.

6. Respect the Audience

"The consumer is not a moron," advertising legend David Ogilvy once said. "She is your wife." He may also be your husband or your significant other, but the point is as true today as it was when Ogilvy made it several decades ago. Yet many of the earliest attempts at integrating brands into entertainment content seemed to willfully ignore the audience, putting the advertisers' needs ahead of those of the consumers of the content.

As digital technologies empower consumers, they are changing the model from intrusion to invitation.

In the intrusive model, it was important for advertisers to be polite guests precisely because they had not been invited in and therefore needed to display good manners. In the new model, advertisers don't even have that choice. If they don't respect the consumer, they'll never get in the door to begin with. Content creators and brand marketers will have to choose partners and projects carefully. Integration will have to be subtle and seamless, and appear natural to the audience. Those integration efforts that are forced will stand out like sore thumbs and will be rejected. Those that work will begin with the consumer in mind and with the goal of creating compelling content, but will still manage to meet the needs of both the advertiser and the creators of the content.

It's called win-win, and it's the ultimate measure of success.

Epilogue

The setting was familiar, but the message was new. Once again, a cross section of entertainment and advertising executives had packed into the sold-out ballroom of the Beverly Hills Hotel on a February morning, this time for the second Madison & Vine conference.

The keynote speaker this time: John Hayes, global chief marketing officer at American Express, a company that had already made a number of forays into branded entertainment and planned more, including a series of mini Internet films directed by Barry Levinson, starring the comedian Jerry Seinfeld and an animated Superman character.

"We act in the marketing communications marketplace by voting with our wallets," Hayes said. "The bottom line is this—the traditional network television business is in enormous transition. The next generation media consumer will redefine the new rules even before they are written, leaving marketers and communications companies more challenged than ever before.... We are continually looking for new and innovative opportunities. For an organization to learn, it must be willing to take risks and freely accept the consequences, good or bad."

If year one was about grand pronouncements and philosophical debates, year two was more grounded, as speaker after speaker—they included Mark Burnett, creator of *Survivor* and the popular Donald Trump reality series *The Apprentice*, and Michael Browner, who controlled General Motors' $3 billion media budget—focused on real-world initiatives and results, and the lessons learned from their successes and failures.

The main themes that emerged from the day: marketers need to set aside budgets to explore branded entertainment; they need to experiment; and they need to accept the inevitable breakdown of their traditional business models and embrace change.

"If you're not willing to fall on your face," said Burnett, "you'll get nothing." Burnett said he was one of the few TV producers enthusiastic about working with advertisers and that he felt it gave him an advantage. He also said that he had been able to protect the integrity of his programs for viewers even while doing product integration deals.

"The financial model is radically changing," Burnett said. "If you don't embrace Madison Avenue and don't recognize that these people are making movies in 30 seconds and selling millions of dollars worth of stuff, you just don't get it."

Criticizing advertisers for paying more money to reach fewer TV viewers, American Express' Hayes noted, "The definition of insanity is to continually do the same thing over and over and expect different results."

Brad Ball, head of corporate marketing for Warner Bros. and a former marketing executive at McDonald's, went a step further, recommending that marketers pull 10 percent of their money out of the network TV upfront market and dedicate it to branded entertainment initiatives. Just over a month later, Ball put his money where his mouth was when he announced he would leave the studio to form his own branded entertainment consultancy, Ball Entertainment Group.

The message that came through most clearly was this: stop talking, start taking risks. Learn from failure, reap the benefits of success. With apologies to Nike, Hollywood and Madison Avenue were repeatedly urged to "Just Do It." The future of marketing and media could hinge on whether they heed that advice.

Notes

Chapter 1

"Coca-Cola spends more than half a billion dollars a year"... Leading National Advertisers Special Report, *Advertising Age*, June 23, 2003

"Like most revolutions...this one is about control"... "Seeking The Next TV Revolution? Here's The Clue: It's Spelled TiVo," by Randall Rothenberg, *Advertising Age*, June 5, 2000

Chapter 2

"A deal involving the ABC soap opera *All My Children*"..."TV Plot Placement Yields ABC A Big Advertising Buy," by Joe Flint and Emily Nelson, *The Wall Street Journal*, March 15, 2002

"Miramax went out to the market asking a record $35 million"... "Green Hornet Shops For A Car," by Richard Linnett and Wayne Friedman, *Advertising Age*, May 26, 2003

"For an NBC reality series called *The Restaurant*"... "Brands Eat At Rocco's," by Hillary Chura and Tobi Elkin, *Advertising Age's Madison & Vine*, July 2, 2003

"Good Charlotte's 'The Anthem' was made available on the video game" ... "By The Demo: Music For The Ages," by Kate Fitzgerald, *Advertising Age*, July 28, 2003

"Ford seemed to have scored a coup"... "Product integrators tackle learning curve," by Wayne Friedman, *Advertising Age*, Oct. 21, 2002

"The two types of ads that consumers were least likely to skip"... "PVR users skip most ads: study," by Wayne Friedman, *Advertising Age*, July 1, 2002

Chapter 4

"The time is the present and the subject is the digital revolution"... "As Interactive Media's Growth Parallels That Of TV's, Fear Of Unknown Slows Advertisers," by Scott Donaton, *Advertising Age*, Feb. 28, 1995

"None of the first four hundred radio stations launched in the United States carried advertising"... *The Sponsor: Notes on Modern Potentates*, by Erik Barnouw, *Transaction Publishers*, 2004 (Originally published by Oxford University Press, 1978)

"Broadcasting's real birth"... "The Advertising Century," by Randall Rothenberg, *Advertising Age*, March 29, 1999

"Some of the aura that surrounds the agency"... "A Global Goliath," by John McDonough, *Advertising Age*, Nov. 2, 1998

"The soap opera was a tremendous vehicle"... "Creating A Brand Management System Was Only The Start Of A Legacy," by Jack Neff, *Advertising Age*, Dec. 13, 1999

"Hazel Bishop...sales soared a hundredfold"..."The Advertising Century," by Randall Rothenberg, *Advertising Age*, March 29, 1999

Chapter 5

"More U.S. homes have outhouses than Tivos," by Bradley Johnson, *Advertising Age*, Nov. 4, 2002

"According to a study by the Yankee Group"..."PVRs to hit 20% by '07," by Hank Kim, *Advertising Age*, Sept. 29, 2003

"Users skipped commercials"..."PVR users skip most ads: study," by Wayne Friedman, *Advertising Age*, July 1, 2002

"In the 1950 broadcast season"..."The Influentials," by Ed Keller and Jon Berry, *The Free Press*, 2003

Chapter 6

"The market value of a ticket to attend the 2003 Victoria's Secret Holiday Fashion Show"..."Some Men Would Do Just About Anything To Be Invited To This," by Shelly Branch, *The Wall Street Journal*, Nov. 13, 2003

"ABC made a similar deal"..."On ABC, Sears Pays To Be Star Of New Series," by Stuart Elliott, *The New York Times*, Dec. 3, 2003

"When the media-buying giant Mindshare"..."Unit Of WPP Will Own Stake In ABC Shows," By Brian Steinberg and Emily Nelson, *The Wall Street Journal*, Dec. 1, 2003

Chapter 7

"Time Warner Cable began to offer DVR functionality"..."Can Cable Fast-Forward Past TiVo?" by Seth Schiesel, *The New York Times*, Oct. 20, 2003

Chapter 8

"In 1980, there were 17,590 screens"...Motion Picture Association: Worldwide Market Research, U.S. Entertainment Industry: 2002 MPA Market Statistics

"Marketing costs rose sharply"...Motion Picture Association: Worldwide Market Research, U.S. Entertainment Industry: 2002 MPA Market Statistics

Chapter 9

"The best car commercial ever"... "Italian Job Gets Big Mileage From Small Cars," by Joe Morgenstern, *The Wall Street Journal*, May 30, 2003

"Dr. Seuss's *The Cat in the Hat* hit theaters"... "Buy This Or That! From Cat In The Hat" by Caroline E. Mayer, *The Washington Post*, Nov. 21, 2003

"General Motors' Pontiac tied in"... "Pontiac's 'XXX' DVD Tie-In Scores Big," by Jean Halliday, *Advertising Age's Madison & Vine*, Feb. 19, 2003

"The film earned a PG-13 rating"... "Coors Under Fire For PG-13 Movie Tie-Ins," by Kate MacArthur, *Advertising Age*, Nov. 3, 2003

"Revolution Studios formed a similar nonexclusive alliance with Ford"... "A Ford Branded Revolution," by T.L.Stanley and Jean Halliday, *Advertising Age's Madison & Vine*, Nov. 5, 2003

"Jeep created three special vehicles"... "Jeep Taps Lara Croft As Its Spokeswoman," by Richard Linnett, *Advertising Age*, March 24, 2003

"Shmuger, though, is among those who believe"... "Universal Asks Brands: Can We Be Co-Creators?" by T.L. Stanley, *Advertising Age*, Nov. 24, 2003

Chapter 10

"The luxury automaker had become trapped"... "BMW Films Deliver," by Kate MacArthur and Jean Halliday, *Advertising Age's Madison & Vine*, Nov. 6, 2002

"It's a nice gesture"... "Cannes Fest Can Recognize Mad & Vine Is Not Just A Fad," by Scott Donaton, *Advertising Age*, June 16, 2003

Chapter 12

"The troubles began midway through 1999"... "The High Cost of Sharing," by Nick Wingfield and Ethan Smith, *The Wall Street Journal*, Sept. 9, 2003, and "Music Industry Presses Play on Plan To Save Its Business," by Bruce Orwall, Martin Peers and Ethan Smith, *The Wall Street Journal*, Sept. 9, 2003

"At its peak, Napster recorded"… "Marketing Tackles Download Mess," by Tobi Elkin, *Advertising Age*, July 28, 2003

"A 2003 study by Edison Media Research"…"Destined To Duet: Music & Marketing," by Marc Pollack, *Advertising Age*, July 28, 2003

"The third path is price cuts"… "Universal Music To Cut CD Prices To Under $13," by Derek Caney, Reuters, Sept. 3, 2003

Chapter 13

"Advertising has become the music industry's new favorite suitor"…"Destined To Duet: Music & Marketing," by Marc Pollack, *Advertising Age*, July 28, 2003

"They show a commercial on TV with Celine Dion"… "Chrysler Sticks With Dion For Fall Launches," by Richard Linnett, *Advertising Age*, July 14, 2003

Chapter 15

"Fill the stage with Lincolns"… "In Return For Big Ford Ad Dollars, 'Tonight Show' To Feature Lincolns," by Suzanne Vranica, *The Wall Street Journal*, April 1, 2002

"In 2000, it was ABC that crossed the line"… "Hosts Of ABC's 'The View' Praise Campbell Soup In Eight Paid Spots," by Shelly Branch, *The Wall Street Journal*, Nov. 14, 2000

"Dodge finally pulled out"… "Dodge Drops Super Bowl Lingerie Plans," by Jean Halliday, AdAge.com, Dec. 17, 2003

Chapter 16

"We're like the Swiss"... "Hollywood Power Trio Sets Up Shop," by Hank Kim, *Advertising Age*, March 24, 2003

"Nexus of the intersection"... "Hollywood's IEP And The Firm To Merge," by Hank Kim, AdAge.com, March 19, 2004

Chapter 17

"iTVX was one of the early players... "Trying To Price Placement," by Louis Chunovic, *Television Week*, Dec. 2, 2002

"Philip Guarascio, an IAG board member"... "IAG To Measure Brand Integration," by Hank Kim, *Advertising Age*, Oct. 27, 2003

Index

About the Author

Scott Donaton is the editor of *Advertising Age*, the world's leading advertising, marketing, and media publication. It was here that he coined the term Madison & Vine, introduced the weekly e-mail newsletter of the same name, and launched the successful Madison & Vine conference. Donaton's work has won various editorial awards, and in 2003 he was inducted into the Advertising Hall of Achievement. He is a frequent and popular speaker at leading industry events and conferences and has made numerous media appearances, including on NBC's *Today* and other television and radio network news programs.